Going Places is dedicated, as always,
to the students of Green Acres School.

Contents

Editors' Note..*vii*

Introduction ....*ix*

1   Starting Out...1
Sightseeing/Tours
Public Transportation

2   Main Sights in Washington, DC..7
On the National Mall
On Capitol Hill
Around Town

3   Main Sights in Maryland..37

4   Main Sights in Virginia...49

5   The Great Outdoors...59
In Maryland
In Virginia
Battlefields/Historic Sites
Pick Your Own
Gardens
Regional Parks and Playgrounds
Nature Centers, Planetariums,
and Sanctuaries
Historical Farms

6   Sports and Recreation..101
Spectator Sports
Canoeing, Kayaking & Sailing
Equestrian
Golfing and Mini-Golf

7   Arts and Entertainment..111
Festivals

8   Books and Toys..129

9   Skating, Boarding and Blading................................135

10 Snowboarding and Skiing..143

11 Swimming and Splashing..145

12 Indoor Recreation..153
Bowling
Indoor Play
Indoor Climbing
Make-Your-Own Art Studios
Laser Tag And Arcades
Sweet Treats

13 Day Trips...163
Annapolis
Baltimore
Chesapeake Bay/Western Maryland
Virginia
Harpers Ferry, West Virginia
Pennsylvania

14 Field Trips...195
Pre-Kindergarten
Kindergarten
First & Second Grade
Third Grade
Fourth Grade
Fifth & Sixth Grade

Index...203

Editors' Note

It is with great pleasure that we welcome you to the 18th Edition of *Going Places with Children in Washington, DC*. Green Acres School has been publishing this wonderful resource since 1958.

We have enjoyed the year spent working to update this book for its new edition. The Washington, DC area offers a wonderfully rich environment for children and families, and our research has led us back to old favorites and on toward new discoveries. We hope that this guide will also help your families explore the arts, history, education, sports, natural beauty and sheer fun of our city.

Please know that this guide is not designed to be an exhaustive list of all the things to do with children in the Washington, DC area, but is a collection of favorite places and activities recommended by the many families, staff, and friends who have been a part of the Green Acres community through our 80 year history.

We would like to thank Annie Groat, Director of Institutional Advancement at Green Acres School, Jill Jackson, and Quinn Smith '11 for helping us to shepherd this project through to completion. We would also like to thank Kara Combs, the staff, teachers, and of course students who contributed ideas, artwork, and quotes for this new edition. We gratefully acknowledge the editors of prior editions of this book. We could not have accomplished this task without the exemplary work of those that preceded us in this role.

Finally, we want to encourage you to make sure to get in touch with all of the places you plan to visit directly. There can always be changes in schedule, hours, availability, and a variety of other variables. Therefore making sure to contact the institution or location directly is always highly recommended.

We hope that you enjoy this book as much as we have enjoyed putting it together. If you have any thoughts or comments to help us improve future editions please feel free to email us at GoingPlaces@greenacres.org.

Brian Roach, Lauren Boyle, and Jennifer Lowe

OCTOBER 2014

Introduction

For the past 80 years, Green Acres School has been dedicated to nurturing children's natural curiosity about the world around them. Through authentic, hands-on experiences on campus and across the greater Washington, DC metro area, our students develop vital skills and understandings. Moreover, they come to see learning as deeply rewarding and engaging, and this intrinsic motivation sets them up for a life of initiative, discovery, and personal and professional satisfaction and success.

Going Places with Children in Washington, DC reflects our strong belief that visiting places outside of the classroom is vital for children's development, and we are proud to share this 18th edition with you. In fact, field trips over many years by Green Acres students formed the basis for several of the places to visit described in these pages. Just as our students have benefited from these experiences, so too do we hope that your children will as well.

Schools, however, are not typically set up to serve simultaneously as publishing houses, and so I am particularly grateful for the leadership of our wonderful editors, Brian Roach, Lauren Boyle, and Jennifer Lowe, as well as the terrific support of Annie Groat, our Director of Institutional Advancement. Of course *Going Places*, as it has always been, is a collaborative, community endeavor, and we are indebted to the parents, teachers, staff members, and students who made this edition possible. We could not have completed it without so many community members' hard work and enthusiasm for this project.

Enjoy *Going Places* while you enrich the lives of your children.

Neal M. Brown
Head of School

OCTOBER 2014

Starting Out

There are several keys to a successful family outing—whether for the afternoon, the weekend, or longer: advance planning, stopping for rest and food, and finding that key balance between planned activities and free time. We've probably all had that experience of pushing the kids too far! The resources below can help you to plan a successful outing with your family!

As always, please note that locations, hours, and fees are subject to change, so please check critical information before you go!

Alexandria Convention and Visitor's Bureau

> 221 King Street
> Alexandria VA 22314
> www.visitalexandriava.com
> 703.746.3301

This Visitor's Center is in the restored home of William Ramsay, Scottish merchant and city founder. Stop here for information on historic Old Town Alexandria. You can also pick up annotated maps, lists of galleries and shops, and tour information.

Annapolis Conference Center and Visitor's Bureau

> 26 West Street
> Annapolis MD 21401
> www.visitannapolis.org
> 410.280.0445

While not a destination in and of itself, the Visitor's Bureau is brimming with free information about the city of Annapolis and many sites in Anne Arundel County. Because there is plenty to see in this area, a stop here can help you plan a visit to meet your family's needs.

Baltimore Visitor Center

401 Light Street
Baltimore MD 21202
www.baltimore.org/visitor-center
877.225.8466

Baltimore is less than a one-hour drive or train ride from Washington, DC. The new White House Visitor's Center is due to reopen in September 2014. Please visit www.nps.gov/whho/planyourvisit/hours.htm for more information. See Chapter 13, "Day Trips," for suggested sights to see, and request a visitor information packet online.

Ellipse Visitor's Pavilion

15th and E Streets NW
Washington DC 20001
www.nps.gov/whho/planyourvisit/hours.htm

This is a temporary visitor's center as of the publication of this book. The new White House Visitor's Center is due to reopen in September 2014. Please visit www.nps.gov/whho/planyourvisit/hours.htm for more information.

Maryland Tourism

411 East Pratt Street, 14th Floor
Baltimore MD 21202
visitmaryland.org/Pages/MarylandHome.aspx
800.634.7386

Call or write to receive a free travel kit, which includes a state map, a calendar of events, and a Destination Maryland Travel Guide.

Senate House and Visitor's Galleries

www.visitthecapitol.gov

Elected officials will often meet with their young constituents and even have a picture taken with the group on the steps of the Capitol, but you must arrange this in writing before your trip. If you are planning to visit Washington in the busy spring season, be sure to make arrangements six months prior to your visit. Gallery passes are required to attend sessions of either legislative body.

Smithsonian Institution Information Center (The Castle)

1000 Jefferson Drive SW
Washington DC 20560
www.si.edu/Museums/smithsonian-institution-building
202.632.1000

Home to the Smithsonian Information Center (see "The Castle" page 14) as well as the Institution's administrative headquarters.

Virginia Tourism Corporation

901 East Byrd Street
Richmond VA 23219
www.virginia.org
800.847.4882

Official tourism website for the Commonwealth of Virginia.

Washington, DC Convention and Visitors Association

1212 New York Avenue NW
Washington DC 20001
www.washington.org
202.789.7000

Get free maps of Washington, brochures on major attractions and special exhibits, hotel information, and a calendar of events.

SIGHTSEEING/TOURS

While there is certainly no shortage of resources available online, sometimes real-life tour guides can greatly enrich your experience when visiting Washington and the surrounding areas. The stories and local information shared by knowledgeable tour guides can provide memorable introduction to the sites, and a multi-stop tour can help you squeeze in a few more sites during a day's visit.

A Tour de Force

PO Box 2782
Washington DC 20013
www.atourdeforce.com
703.535.2948

Enjoy specially designed, historically oriented tours of Washington, DC neighborhoods, monuments, and museums. Each tour is filled with stories of the people who have made Washington such an impressive national capital city.

DC Duck Tours

2640 Reed Street NE
Washington DC 20018
www.dcducks.com
202.832.9800

Take a land/water tour on an amphibious vehicle. The "Ducks" are the same ones that were used to carry troops and supplies in World War II and are fully restored and Coast Guard approved. The fully narrated tour spends one hour on land and 30 minutes on the water. Children are sure to be thrilled when the "bus" drives into the Potomac River!

Old Town Trolley Tours (DC)

50 Massachusetts Avenue NE
Washington DC 20002
www.trolleytours.com/washington-dc
202.832.9800

Old Town Trolley Tours offers a wide-ranging tour of 100 points of interest in Washington, including Georgetown, Embassy Row, the Washington National Cathedral, Capitol Hill, Dupont Circle, and the Mall. Passengers can get off and re-board at their leisure at 18 stops. The ride in an old-fashioned trolley car makes sightseeing all the more enjoyable. Out of town visitors—check to see if the trolleys stop near your hotel. Evening tours are available by reservation.

Potomac Riverboat Company Cruises

205 The Strand
Alexandria VA 22314
www.potomacriverboatco.com
703.684.0580

The Admiral Tip offers a 40-minute narrated cruise along the waterfront of historic Alexandria. The Matthew Hayes is a 90-minute narrated cruise past Washington's monuments. Miss Christin provides roundtrip transportation to Mount Vernon, home of George Washington—upon arrival at the estate, you will take a land tour of the grounds, gardens, and museums.

Spirit Cruises

600 Water Street SW
Washington DC 20024
www.spiritcruises.com
866.404.8439

Both Spirit of Washington and Potomac Spirit operate from Pier 4 in Washington, DC. Spirit of Washington offers two-hour lunch cruises, three-hour dinner cruises, and two-and-a-half-hour evening and moonlight cruises. Sights along the route include the Capitol and historic monuments, Fort McNair, Reagan National Airport, and the Potomac skyline.

Washington Walks

819 G Street SW
Washington DC 20024
www.washingtonwalks.com
202.484.1565

Since 1999, Washington Walks guides have been leading visitors and locals alike along the streets of America's capital city, revealing the stories and sites that abound on the National Mall and beyond. The walking tours require no reservations, take place rain or shine, and are reasonably priced. Most of the walk routes are wheelchair accessible.

PUBLIC TRANSPORTATION

Many of the sites in *Going Places* are readily accessible by public transportation. Like many other big cities, Washington, DC and its surrounding areas can be challenging to navigate by car. So you may want to leave the driving and parking hassles at home and try the region's extensive public transportation system. Kids often find public transportation itself to be another fun activity.

DASH

www.dashbus.com

DASH operates buses along four routes within the City of Alexandria, Virginia, connecting several Metrorail stations with locations throughout the city, including the Old Town shopping and restaurant area.

MARC Trains

www.mta.maryland.gov/marc-train

This commuter rail service links DC with Baltimore and points in Maryland and West Virginia. All three lines have their Washington, DC terminal at Union Station. These trains operate on weekdays only, about every half hour during the commuter rush and approximately every hour otherwise. Weekly and monthly tickets are available.

MARC and VRE (Virginia Railway Express) tickets to Washington are good for travel on one another's trains that leave Washington before noon and arrive in Washington after noon.

Tickets are available by mail.

Metrorail and Metrobus

www.wmata.com

Parking in many downtown areas is expensive and difficult to find. Avoid frustration by using Metro, Washington's subway and bus system.

Northern Virginia Transportation Commission

www.thinkoutsidethecar.org

Contact this organization for information on other mass transit options in Northern Virginia. Some are designed to serve commuters, others may be of interest to visitors to Washington, DC.

Ride-On Buses (Montgomery County, MD)

www.montgomerycountymd.gov/dot-transit/index.html

The blue and white Ride-On buses are part of the transportation network in Montgomery County, MD. They stop only at the blue and white Ride-On signs. Day passes are available, and Metrobus transfers are valid on Ride-On buses.

Virginia Railway Express

www.vre.org

This commuter rail service links DC with Virginia. The trains operate weekdays only, coming into Washington in the morning and leaving Washington in the afternoon and evening. Use a credit card to purchase tickets at the stations or via the Internet.

Main Sights in Washington, DC

Washington, DC is home not only to the three branches of the United States government and to the monuments and museums surrounding the National Mall, but to a wonderful collection of historical and cultural resources of its own. As our country's capital city, Washington is host to embassies and organizations from around the world—and it is a city rich in the fine and performing arts, in natural resources, and in recreational opportunities. The sights and museums in this section express the enormous diversity of the city, from the National Mall to Capitol Hill and to the city beyond.

ON THE NATIONAL MALL

The National Mall is the heart of Washington, home to many of the monuments, museums and main attractions that draw visitors to the nation's capital. The Mall is almost two miles of open space and there is no such thing as a quick walk from one end to the other, especially in the heat of summer. A good stroller is a must for young children, as are comfortable shoes for everyone else.

On a beautiful day, pick two or three museums to visit for an hour or two. You can take a break or picnic at the carousel near the Air and Space Museum, in the two marvelous sculpture gardens near the Hirshhorn and at the National Gallery of Art, and at the outdoor fountain at the East Wing.

A visit to the Smithsonian Information Center, in the Castle, will provide you with an orientation to all 15 Smithsonian locations in Washington, including the National Zoo (see page 29).

Admission to all museums on the Mall is free. Parking on Mall streets is very limited, so use Metrorail if possible. Otherwise, try your luck or find a nearby parking garage.

Constitution Gardens

Between the Washington Monument and the Lincoln Memorial on Constitution Avenue NW
Washington DC 20024
www.nps.gov/coga
202.426.6841

A large mall area, on which temporary government buildings once stood, has been transformed into a memorial to the Founders of the United States. The informal design includes a six-acre lake with a landscaped island (the site of the 56 Signers of the Declaration of Independence Memorial). The unusual design was intended to create the effect of a park within a park. This is a pleasant place to stop and take a break from sightseeing. Take a stroll, play some outdoor games, and give the children a chance to stretch their legs.

Franklin Delano Roosevelt Memorial

1850 West Basin Drive SW
Washington DC 20242
www.nps.gov/frde/index.htm
202.426.6841
Metrorail Blue and Orange lines (Smithsonian)

This memorial creates the sense of a secluded garden. Surrounded by shade trees, waterfalls, and quiet alcoves, the memorial is divided into four outdoor galleries separated by walls of red South Dakota granite, featuring quotations from Franklin Delano Roosevelt.

Freer Sackler/The Smithsonian's Museum of Asian Art

1050 Independence Avenue NW
Washington DC 20013
www.asia.si.edu
202.633.1000
Metrorail Blue and Orange lines (Smithsonian)

In an underground quadrangle formed by the Arts and Industries Building and the Freer Gallery, this museum of Asian art is connected to the Freer by underground exhibition areas. The Sackler Gallery houses one of the finest collections of Asian art, including ancient Chinese jades and bronzes and important Chinese paintings. It also offers a schedule of interesting loan exhibitions.

Chinese jades, bronzes, and paintings, Buddhist sculpture, Japanese screens, early Biblical manuscripts, miniatures from India and Persia are exhibited at the distinguished Asian collection at the Freer. Exhibits are continuously rotated since only a fraction of the catalogued artwork can be displayed at one time. The Freer is also noted for its collection of important work by American artists, especially James Whistler. Whistler's "Peacock Room," with its lavish golds and blues, will particularly fascinate children. ImaginAsia, a hands-on art project for adults and children, takes place on Saturdays in the spring, weekdays in the summer and Saturdays in the fall.

Hirshhorn Museum and Sculpture Garden

700 Independence Avenue SW
Washington DC 20560
www.hirshhorn.si.edu
202.633.4674
Metrorail Blue and Orange lines (Smithsonian), Blue/Green/Orange and Yellow lines (L'Enfant Plaza)

This monumental collection of 19th- and 20th-century paintings and sculpture, displayed in an unusual circular building, offers children an exciting introduction to art. Many of the paintings are massive, vivid, and often very colorful—making a direct impact on viewers, young and old. Exhibits from the comprehensive permanent collection (nearly 14,500 paintings, sculptures, and works on paper) and changing loan shows provide opportunities to study major modern artists such as Rodin, Calder, Eakins, and Matisse. Diverse art movements, including realism, pop, and abstract expressionism, can be studied in depth.

Jefferson Memorial

Southern edge of the Tidal Basin
Washington DC 20242
www.nps.gov/thje
202.426.6841
Metrorail Blue and Orange lines (Smithsonian)

The pillared rotunda is a tribute to our third President,
Thomas Jefferson, who was also the author of the Declaration
of Independence. Like the Lincoln Memorial, it is impressively
lit at night. Park Service rangers are available to provide visitor
services and present interpretive programs every hour.

Korean War Veterans Memorial

10 Daniel French Drive SW
Washington DC 20001
www.nps.gov/kwvm
202.426.6841
Metrorail Blue and Orange lines (Smithsonian or Foggy Bottom)

A group of 19 stainless-steel statues, created by World War II
veteran Frank Gaylord, depicts a squad on patrol and evokes
the experience of American ground troops in Korea. Strips of
granite and scrubby juniper bushes suggest the rugged Korean
terrain, while windblown ponchos recall the harsh weather. This
symbolic patrol brings together members of the U.S. Air Force,
Army, Marines, and Navy; the men portrayed are from a variety
of ethnic backgrounds.

Lincoln Memorial

2 Lincoln Memorial Circle NW
Washington DC 20037
www.nps.gov/linc
202.426.6841
Metrorail Blue and Orange lines (Smithsonian or Foggy Bottom)

This classical Greek memorial to the Great Emancipator, Abraham
Lincoln, is one of the most beautiful sights in Washington.
Thirty-six marble columns, representing the 36 states of the
Union at the time of Lincoln's death, surround the impressive
seated statue of Lincoln. Passages from two of his great
speeches, the Second Inaugural Address and the Gettysburg
Address, are carved on the walls. At the foot of the memorial
is the 2,000-foot-long Reflecting Pool, which mirrors the

Washington Monument at its other end. Try to visit the Lincoln Memorial twice—once in the daytime and once at night.

Martin Luther King Jr. Memorial

1964 Independence Avenue SW
Washington DC 20024
www.nps.gov/mlkm
202.426.6841
Metrorail Blue and Orange lines (Smithsonian)

The newest structure on the National Mall, the MLK Jr. Memorial opened in August 2011, on the 48th anniversary of the March on Washington. The memorial is located on a 4-acre site that borders the Tidal Basin. The memorial is near the Franklin Delano Roosevelt Memorial and is intended to create a visual "line of leadership" from the Lincoln Memorial, on whose steps King gave his "I Have a Dream" speech at the March on Washington, to the Jefferson Memorial. The centerpiece for the memorials is a 30 foot sculpture of King named the "Stone of Hope" which stands past two other pieces of granite that symbolize the "Mountain of Despair." Visitors literally "pass through" the Mountain of Despair on the way to the Stone of Hope, symbolically "moving through the struggle as Dr. King did during his life."

National Air and Space Museum

601 Independence Avenue NW
Washington DC 20597
www.nasm.si.edu
202.633.2211
Metrorail Blue and Orange lines (Smithsonian)

A place where you can see everything that flies.
NICOLE, AGE 9

This great aerospace center has 26 exhibit areas, a puppet theater, film theater, and planetarium. The central display on "Milestones of Flight" includes: the Wright brothers' Flyer of 1903, the "X-1," the first plane to break the sound barrier, Lindbergh's Spirit of St. Louis, and the command module of the Apollo 11 moon-landing mission. In another section, children can walk through the Skylab orbital workshop and examine the astronauts' living and lab quarters. Each gallery explores a different theme: helicopters, satellites, World War I and II planes, rockets, and more. Many exhibits use motion pictures or a moving display to explain a particular subject. To avoid crowds, go early on a weekday morning or late in the evening during extended summer hours. Purchase film tickets when you arrive as the day's showing can be sold out quickly.

National Archives

700 Pennsylvania Avenue NW
Washington DC 20408
www.archives.gov
866.272.6272
Metrorail Blue and Orange lines (Federal Triangle)
Green and Yellow lines (Archives)

This is the repository of America's records and documents. Permanently on display (and also available online) are the nation's three great charters of freedom: the Declaration of Independence, the Constitution, and the Bill of Rights. These documents are kept in sealed glass and bronze cases, which are lowered every night into a bomb-and-fireproof vault 20 feet below floor level. Other documents are displayed on a rotating basis in the Exhibition Hall.

National Gallery of Art

401 Constitution Avenue NW
Washington DC 20565
www.nga.gov
202.737.4215
Metrorail Blue and Orange lines (Federal Triangle)
Green and Yellow lines (Archives)

> *...the coolest art.*
> NICOLE, AGE 9

One of the world's great art museums, the National Gallery contains major collections of European and American paintings and sculpture. Among its Renaissance and Dutch paintings are masterpieces by Raphael, Rembrandt, and Titian. The gallery hosts major loan shows from around the world in addition to its own special exhibits. The West Building's main foyer is huge and awe-inspiring. Loud whispers can be heard around its circular indoor fountain. The beautiful, light filled East Building, designed by I.M. Pei, houses the modern and contemporary collections. Don't miss the underground concourse connecting the two buildings, with its light sculpture, moving walkway, cool fountain view, café, and gift shop. The outdoor sculpture garden hosts concert series in the summer, and ice skating in winter. For a tour of the main collection, children do well with an audio tour. For a small fee, recorded tours are also available for most major exhibits.

National Museum of African Art

950 Independence Avenue NW
Washington DC 20560
www.africa.si.edu
202.633.4600
Metrorail Blue and Orange lines (Smithsonian)

Located in the Smithsonian Quadrangle building next to the Arthur M. Sackler Gallery and the Smithsonian Arts and Industries Building, this underground structure is devoted to the collection, study, and display of the traditional and contemporary arts of the entire African continent. Its exhibitions are drawn from the museum's collection of 7,000 African art objects in wood, metal, clay, ivory, and fiber.

National Museum of American History

1300 Constitution Avenue NW
Washington DC 20560
www.americanhistory.si.edu
202.633.1000
Metrorail Blue and Orange lines (Federal Triangle, Smithsonian)

Massive and modern outside, spacious and fascinating inside, this Smithsonian building is the home of the original Star-Spangled Banner and the gowns of our nation's First Ladies. The diversity of the collection makes this museum appealing to children and adults of all ages.

National Museum of Natural History

10th Street and Constitution Avenue NW
Washington DC 20560
www.mnh.si.edu
202.633.1000
Metrorail Blue and Orange lines (Federal Triangle, Smithsonian)

It's hard to decide where to begin a visit to this incredible Smithsonian center for the study of humans and their natural environment. The fossils (highlighted by reconstructions of dinosaur skeletons), mammals (animals in lifelike settings), sea life (a living coral reef and 92-foot blue whale model), and birds are all worthwhile choices. Children are dazzled by the gem and mineral collections that include the world-famous Hope Diamond in the newly renovated Hall of Geology, Gems, and Minerals. Consider using the museum's new Qrius School

Programs for an interesting interactive experience. More information at www.qrius.si.edu

National Museum of the American Indian

Independence Avenue SW
Washington DC 20560
www.nmai.si.edu
202.633.6644
Metrorail Blue, Green, Orange and Yellow lines (L'Enfant Plaza)

The National Museum of the American Indian houses one of the world's largest and most diverse collections of its kind. The museum's sweeping curvilinear architecture, its indigenous landscaping, and its exhibitions, all designed in collaboration with tribes and communities from across the hemisphere, combine to give visitors from around the world the sense and spirit of Native America.

Smithsonian Institution Information Center (The Castle)

1000 Jefferson Drive SW
Washington DC 20260
www.si.edu
202.633.1000
Metrorail Blue and Orange lines (Smithsonian)

For the visitor who wishes to be introduced to the 14 Smithsonian museums and the National Zoo in Washington, the Castle is the place to start. This aptly named building was the first of the Smithsonians, designed by James Renwick, Jr. and completed in 1855. Today, it houses the Smithsonian Information Center. There are two orientation theaters that continuously show a 20-minute video overview of the Institution, "touch screen" programs in six languages on the Smithsonian museums and on other capital highlights, two electronic wall maps, and scale models of famous Washington monuments. The "touch screen" programs and electronic maps are very appealing to children. To receive a packet of information to help plan your visit to the Smithsonian, write to Smithsonian Information or e-mail info@si.edu.

U.S. Botanic Garden

100 Maryland Avenue SW
Washington DC 20024
www.usbg.gov
202.225.8333
Metrorail Blue and Orange lines (Federal Center)

The United States Botanic Garden is the oldest botanic garden in North America. The garden highlights the diversity of plants worldwide, as well as their aesthetic, cultural, economic, therapeutic, and ecological significance. The complex includes the Conservatory, the Frederick Auguste Bartholdi Park with its historic fountain of sea nymphs and monsters, the newly created three-acre site of the National Garden, and the DC Village Production Facility—a nursery and greenhouse complex responsible for producing all the USBG plants as well as many for Capitol Hill. Public programs offered include classes, information on gardening and botany, tours for school children, and special exhibits.

Vietnam Veterans Memorial

5 Henry Bacon Drive NW
Washington DC 20024
www.nps.gov/vive
202.426.6841
Metrorail Blue and Orange lines (Foggy Bottom)

This memorial to Vietnam Veterans was dedicated November 13, 1982. The design by Maya Ying Lin, then a 21-year old architecture student, consists of two black granite walls set in the ground in a shallow V. The walls are inscribed with over 58,000 names of the dead. At the entrances, books are available to assist visitors in finding specific names. Frederick Hart's life-size sculpture of three soldiers and the Vietnam Women's Memorial designed by Glenda Goodace are also part of this memorial. Set in the peaceful, contemplative surroundings of Constitution Gardens, the Vietnam Veterans Memorial imparts a powerful sense of loss. People touch and make rubbings of the names and leave tokens of every description. Be prepared to answer difficult questions from children about the Vietnam War.

Washington Monument

2 15th Street NW
Washington DC 20007
www.nps.gov/wamo
202.426.6841
Metrorail Blue and Orange lines (Smithsonian)

An impressive obelisk rising 555 feet is our nation's memorial to its founder. A 70-second elevator ride takes visitors to the 500-foot level for a magnificent view of the city.

White House

1600 Pennsylvania Avenue NW
Washington DC 20500
www.whitehouse.gov
202.456.1111
Metrorail Blue and Orange lines (Federal Triangle, McPherson Square)
Red line (Metro Center)

Public tour requests must be submitted through one's Member of Congress. These self-guided tours are available from 7:30 a.m. to 11:30 a.m. Tuesday through Thursday, 7:30 a.m. to 1:30 p.m. Fridays and Saturdays (excluding federal holidays or unless otherwise noted). Tour hours will be extended when possible based on the official White House schedule. Tours are scheduled on a first come, first served basis. Requests can be submitted up to six months in advance and no less than 21 days in advance. You are encouraged to submit your request as early as possible as a limited number of spaces are available. All White House tours are free of charge.

ON CAPITOL HILL

The Capitol

Washington DC 20004
www.visitthecapitol.gov
202.225.6827
Metrorail Blue and Orange lines (Capital South) Red line (Union Station)

Take a 45-minute guided tour of the U.S. Capitol and see all the areas in the Capitol open to the public: the Rotunda, Statuary Hall, original Capitol, Old Senate Chamber, Old Supreme Court Chamber, crypt area, and beautifully decorated Brumidi corridors. The Whispering Gallery is fun for children. To visit the House and Senate Galleries, you must obtain a pass from your Senator or Congressman.

Eastern Market

225 7th Street SE
Washington DC 20003
www.easternmarket-dc.org
202.698.5253
*Metrorail Blue and Orange lines
(Eastern Market)*

*Sample delicious foods
and buy produce
from farmers.*
ELLA, AGE 10

This farmers market, built in 1871, is still a lively produce market. Children enjoy the outdoor event on Saturdays; there is much to look at and much to buy. A number of vendors sell an array of fruits, vegetables, and flowers; other colorful stalls are crowded with jewelry, cotton clothing, wooden toys, African-American art, pottery, and more. Inside, tasty food counters are located downstairs. If the lines are long, try the casual food establishments across the street. Art exhibits and marvelous pottery are located upstairs.

Folger Shakespeare Library

201 East Capitol Street SE
Washington DC 20003
www.folger.edu
202.544.4600
Metrorail Blue and Orange lines (Capitol South) Red line (Union Station)

The Folger Shakespeare Library houses a unique collection of rare books and manuscripts relating to the humanities of the Renaissance and focusing on Shakespeare. Don't miss the Elizabethan Theater, used throughout the year for plays, lectures, concerts, and poetry readings.

Library of Congress

101 Independence Avenue SE
Washington DC 20540
www.loc.gov
202.707.5000
Metrorail Blue and Orange lines (Capital South) Red line (Union Station)

The Library of Congress, the largest literary treasure house in the world, offers a splendid example of Italian Renaissance architecture, with its domed main reading room and beautiful exhibition hall in the Thomas Jefferson Building. The Library's three buildings house 105 million books, maps, manuscripts, photographs, prints, motion pictures, microfilms, and documents. Permanent exhibitions of interest to older children include a Gutenberg Bible and a 15th-century illuminated Bible manuscript. Public exhibitions drawn from the collections change frequently.

National Postal Museum

2 Massachusetts Avenue NE
Washington DC 20002
www.postalmuseum.si.edu
202.633.5555
Metrorail Red line (Union Station)

Housed in a historic 1914 Beaux Arts building, the National Postal Museum is the perfect place to engage school children in a trip through history. Everyone is fascinated by the railway postal car where 600 pieces of mail had to be sorted in an hour, the early mail planes hanging from the ceiling in the central court area, the unusual homemade mailboxes from rural America and around the world, and vehicles used in mail delivery—a stagecoach, a mail truck on a sled, and a Model T with wild snow tires. Self-guided groups may visit any time and may request pre-visit materials by telephone or online.

U.S. Supreme Court

1 First Street NE
Washington DC 20543
www.supremecourt.gov
202.479.3000
Metrorail Blue and Orange lines (Capital South) Red line (Union Station)

This dazzling white marble building dates from 1935 and houses the highest Court in the land. It is a powerful symbol of the third branch of our democratic government. The spectacle of the Court in session is most impressive. Note the bronze doors at the west entrance, depicting scenes in the historic development of law, and the Great Hall with the marble busts of all the former Chief Justices.

AROUND TOWN

The African-American Civil War Memorial and Museum

1925 Vermont Avenue NW
Washington DC 20001
www.afroamcivilwar.org
202.667.2667
Metrorail Green and Yellow lines (U Street, Shaw)

The mission of the African American Civil War Memorial and Museum is to preserve and tell the stories of the United States Colored Troops and African American involvement in the American Civil War. They utilize a rich collection of primary resources, educational programming and technology to create a meaningful learning experience focused on this pivotal time in American history.

Anacostia Museum and Center for African American History and Culture

1901 Fort Place SE
Washington DC 20020
www.anacostia.si.edu
202.633.4820

This museum, run by the Smithsonian Institution, documents the experiences, culture, and heritage of African Americans and people of African descent through paintings, sculpture, and historical documents. Films, slides, and touchable artifacts often accompany exhibits and make for a stimulating museum experience for all. Exhibitions change frequently and include a variety of projects and activities that stress participation from preschool to adult groups. Guided tours are available on Saturdays by reservation. Pre-tour materials are provided for scheduled groups, and teaching kits are available to educators.

Basilica of the National Shrine of the Immaculate Conception

400 Michigan Avenue NE
Washington DC 20017
www.nationalshrine.com
202.526.8300
Metrorail Red line (Brookland/CUA)

This is the largest Roman Catholic Church in the Western Hemisphere. It is an ideal location to introduce children to the majesty and elegance of religious art.

B'nai B'rith Klutznick National Jewish Museum

1120 20th Street NW
Washington DC 20036
www.bnaibrith.org/museum-and-archives.html
202.857.6647
Metrorail Blue and Orange lines (Farragut West) Red line (Farragut North)

This museum encompasses a wide range of Jewish cultural, artistic, historical, and traditional ritual and ceremonial items. Life-cycle events and holidays are featured. Rotating special exhibitions are of particular interest, as are lectures, children's activities, and young members' events. Open only by appointment to view highlights of the collection.

Bureau of Engraving and Printing

14th and C Streets SW
Washington DC 20228
www.moneyfactory.gov
202.874.8888
Metrorail Blue and Orange lines (Smithsonian)

Millions of dollars are printed here daily. The Bureau also prints stamps and other official government financial papers. Visitors watch all the processes involved in producing currency— printing and cutting sheets of special papers and, most impressive, stacking and counting the bills. A recording gives explanations and background information.

Crime and Punishment Museum

575 7th Street NW
Washington DC 20004
www.crimemuseum.org
202.393.1099
Metrorail Green, Red and Yellow lines
(Gallery Place/Chinatown)

> *A museum about law*
> *enforcement, forensic*
> *science, and the*
> *history of crime.*
> ELIAS, AGE 10

Explore American History from a different perspective. The museum features five unique galleries that burrow deep into the studies of criminal intent, criminal profiles, the penal system, victims, crime prevention, forensic science, law enforcement, and the Judiciary Branch of government.

Corcoran Gallery of Art

500 17th Street NW
Washington DC 20006
www.corcoran.org/home
202.639.1700
Metrorail Blue and Orange lines (Farragut West) Red line (Farragut North)
(AT TIME OF PUBLICATION CORCORAN ANNOUNCED A MERGER WITH THE NATIONAL GALLERY OF ART AND GEORGE WASHINGTON UNIVERSITY.)

The Corcoran Gallery is the oldest and largest private museum of art in the nation's capital. Founded in 1869 by William Wilson Corcoran, the museum is dedicated to encouraging American excellence in the fine arts.

Daughters of the American Revolution Museum

1776 D Street NW
Washington, DC 20006
www.dar.org
202.628.1776
Metrorail Blue and Orange lines (Farragut West) Red line (Farragut North)

The Museum, located in DAR headquarters, features two galleries with changing exhibitions of American decorative arts and 33 period rooms. Visit the New Hampshire Attic, where dolls, toys, and children's furniture from the 18th and 19th centuries are displayed. Then visit the parlors, kitchen, and dining rooms, all furnished with fine period objects.

Dumbarton Oaks Gardens and Museum

1703 32nd Street
Washington DC 20007
www.doaks.org
202.339.6400
Metrorail Blue and Orange lines (Foggy Bottom) Red line (Dupont Circle)

Dumbarton Oaks Gardens, an oasis in bustling Georgetown, is spectacular in the spring, beautiful in the fall, and pleasant in the summer and winter. The estate's ten acres of terraced hillsides, formal and informal plantings, and curving footpaths are artfully landscaped, expertly maintained, and enjoyed by children and adults. After viewing the gardens, follow Lover's Lane (on the east border of the gardens) to Dumbarton Oaks Park, a 27-acre wooded, natural area best known for its pools, waterfalls, and spring wildflowers.

Explorers Hall, National Geographic Society

1145 17th Street NW
Washington DC 20036
www.ngmuseum.org
202.857.7700
Metrorail Red line (Farragut North)

Explorers Hall has great appeal to children of all ages. The museum houses a wide variety of temporarily traveling exhibits as well as permanent interactive exhibits. See the website for topics, times, and dates.

Ford's Theatre, Lincoln Museum, Petersen House

511 10th Street NW
Washington DC 20004
www.fordstheatre.org
202.347.4833
Metrorail Blue, Orange and Red lines (Metro Center)

The museum, located in the basement of the theater, provides a self-guided tour that follows Lincoln's career as a lawyer, campaigner, President, and finally, as the victim of an assassin's bullet. Among the memorabilia on display are the clothes Lincoln wore that fatal night. Talks by Park Service rangers describe the events that led up to the assassination.

Franciscan Monastery

1400 Quincy Street NE
Washington DC 20017
www.myfranciscan.org
202.526.6800
Metrorail Red line (Brookland/CUA)

Called the Memorial Church of the Holy Land, this unusual
church is located in a 44-acre woodland. The grounds include
one of the largest rose gardens in the country. Along the garden
walks are the 14 Stations of the Cross with replicas of shrines
in Bethlehem and Lourdes. Children like the catacombs beneath
the church.

Frederick Douglass Home (Cedar Hill)

1411 W Street SE
Washington DC 20020
www.nps.gov/frdo/index.htm
202.426.5960
Metrorail Green line (Anacostia)

The noted orator and anti-slavery editor Frederick Douglass
spent the later years of his life at Cedar Hill. The character
of the fervent abolitionist is reflected in the furnishings of the
house and in information given on regular tours, which cover
14 of 21 rooms. One point of interest is the "Growlery," a
small, one-room structure, separate from the house, to which
Douglass often retreated. Most of the furniture and artwork is
original to the house and is typical of that found in any upper-
middle-class white or African-American home of the late 19th
century. The handsome brick house with its commanding view
of the Federal City is spacious and comfortable by the standards
of the late 19th century.

Hillwood Museum and Garden

4155 Linnean Avenue NW
Washington DC 20008
www.hillwoodmuseum.org
202.686.8500
Metrorail Red line (Van Ness/UDC)

The home of American businesswoman and cereal heiress
Marjorie Merriweather Post boasts among its treasures 90
jeweled items crafted by Faberge. The twenty-five acre estate

in the middle of Washington, DC is home to one of the world's most remarkable collections of 18th and 19th century Russian imperial art outside of Russia, a fascinating collection of French decorative arts, and an impressive house and gardens. A film about Mrs. Post's life precedes the tour and is an excellent introduction to the founder's life and her collections of art.

Historical Society of Washington, DC

801 K Street NW
Washington DC 20001
www.historydc.org
202.249.3955
Metrorail Green and Yellow lines (Mount Vernon Sq/7th St-Convention Center) Green, Red and Yellow lines (Gallery Place/Chinatown)

Local neighborhood stories and the history and culture of the District of Columbia are the focus of this museum, operated by the Historical Society of Washington, DC in the historic DC Central Library Carnegie Building. Changing gallery exhibits devoted to specific Washington, DC communities along with exhibits examining the cultural, historical and recreational life of the city over the past three centuries, along with a multi-media presentation on the history of DC are among the principal features of the museum.

International Spy Museum

800 F Street NW
Washington DC 20004
www.spymuseum.org
202.393.7798
Metrorail Green, Red and Yellow lines (Gallery Place/Chinatown)

> *I like looking at all the gadgets and looking at the cars.*
> CALLUM, AGE 8

The International Spy Museum has a fantastic collection of espionage artifacts from around the world and provides an entertaining look at the role that spies play in current and historical events. The School for Spies exhibit looks at the motivation and skill required for a career in espionage, along with a chance for visitors to try out their proficiency in observation and analysis. In the Spies Among Us exhibit, visitors may be intrigued to find chef Julia Child along with singer Josephine Baker and movie director John Ford.

Islamic Center

2551 Massachusetts Avenue NW
Washington DC 20008
www.theislamiccenter.com
202.332.8343
Metrorail Red line (Dupont Circle)

This mosque is one of the largest and most ornate in the United States. Guides explain the religious service and point out the rich decorations of the building—the rugs, mosaics, and art objects are outstanding examples of Islamic design and craftsmanship. Prayers are held five times daily.

Katzen Arts Center/American University Museum

4400 Massachusetts Avenue NW
Washington DC 20016
www.american.edu/cas/katzen
202.885.1000
Metrorail Red line (Tenleytown/AU)

Permanent exhibitions at the Museum are the University's memorial Watkins collection of modern art and the collection of the representative works in Pop Art (Roy Lichtenstein), Washington art (Gene Davis and Sam Gilliam) and glass sculpture donated to American University by Dr. Cyrus and Myrtle Katzen.

The John F. Kennedy Center for the Performing Arts

2700 F Street NW
Washington DC 20566
www.kennedy-center.org
202.416.8000
*Metrorail Blue and Orange lines
(Foggy Bottom/GWU)*

> *I like that they do lots of great performances and usually in the back room they have a band.*
> ARI, AGE 8.

Performances of music, opera, dance, theater, and film from the United States and abroad are presented on the stages of the Kennedy Center. There are five main theaters: the Concert Hall, Opera House, Eisenhower Theater, Terrace Theater, and Theater Lab. The first three of these theaters is separated by two great parallel halls, one decorated with the flags of the 50 states, and the other with the flags of the nations of the world. Children enjoy these impressive displays. There is an array of children's performances and educational opportunities. Visit the website to learn more.

Koshland Science Museum

525 E Street NW
Washington DC 20001
www.koshland-science-museum.org
202.334.1201
Metrorail Green and Yellow lines (Gallery Place/Chinatown)
Red line (Gallery Place/Chinatown or Judiciary Square)

The Marian Koshland Science Museum of the National
Academy of Sciences engages the public in many of the most
important scientific issues of our time. Interactive displays based
on findings of the National Academy of Sciences illustrate the
roles of science in informing national policy and people's daily
lives. Recent exhibits have included DNA, global warming,
infectious diseases and the wonders of science. The museum
hosts several special events per month, including educational
activities for groups, teachers, and school district coordinators.

The Kreeger Museum

2401 Foxhall Road NW
Washington DC 20007
www.kreegermuseum.org
202.338.3552

The Kreeger Museum, located at the former residence of
Carmen and David Kreeger, contains an impressive collection
of 19th and 20th century paintings and sculptures by such
artists as Picasso, Van Gogh, Monet, Kandinsky, Miro, Rodin,
Stella, and Moore. It also has a broad range of African art and
sculpture. The setting alone is worth the visit!

Lincoln Cottage/President Lincoln
and Soldiers' Home National Monument

140 Rock Creek Church Road NW
Washington DC 20011
www.lincolncottage.org
202.829.0436

During the Civil War, Lincoln resided seasonally on the grounds
of the federally owned Soldiers' Home. Each year from 1862 to
1864, Lincoln commuted daily by horseback or carriage from
the Soldiers' Home to the White House from June through
November. During his first summer in the residence, Lincoln
developed his emancipation policy. Today, the Soldiers' Home
still commands spectacular views of the city.

Madame Tussauds DC

1001 F Street NW
Washington DC 20004
www.madametussauds.com/
washington
202.942.7300
Metrorail Blue, Orange and Red lines (Metro Center)

> *There are many presidents and Justin Bieber, they look so real, especially the eyes.*
> ALEXANDROS, AGE 7

Madame Tussauds Washington, DC features this town's local celebrities—politicians. Former DC Mayor Marion Barry and *Washington Post* reporter Bob Woodward, of Watergate fame, join Barack Obama, Hillary Clinton, George Bush and Richard Nixon, among other local luminaries, in addition to the broader range of famous figures that Madame Tussauds is famous for. The Museum uses touch-screens and recordings to bring to life historic celebrities such as Abraham Lincoln and Rosa Parks.

National Building Museum

401 F Street NW
Washington DC 20001
www.nbm.org
202.272.2448
Metrorail Green, Red and Yellow lines (Judiciary Square, Gallery Place/ Chinatown)

The National Building Museum is America's leading cultural institution devoted to the history and impact of the built environment. Located just four blocks from the National Mall, the Museum occupies a magnificent building with a soaring Great Hall, colossal 75-foot-tall Corinthian columns, and a 1,200-foot terra cotta frieze.

National Museum of Women in the Arts

1250 New York Avenue NW
Washington DC 20005
www.nmwa.org
202.783.5000
Metrorail Blue, Orange and Red lines (Metro Center)

This is a comfortably small museum housing art by women from the 16th century to the present day. Included are works by Mary Cassatt, photographs by Louise Dahl-Wolfe, and sculpture by Camille Claudel. Special exhibits present international women's accomplishments. The galleries in which works are displayed are not too large, so children can wander through them without feeling lost. During the school year, the museum's Education Department offers Sunday children's programs relating to the current exhibition or aspects of the permanent collection. Special tours geared to children ages 6-12 are offered and are often followed by a related hands-on experience. Call for details.

National Portrait Gallery

Eighth and F Streets NW
Washington DC 20001
www.npg.si.edu
202.633.8300
*Metrorail Green, Red and Yellow lines
(Gallery Place/Chinatown)*

Pick a favorite photo exhibit and then have a snack at the café!
ELLA, AGE 10

The National Portrait Gallery examines American history by focusing on the individuals who have aided in the development of our nation. The collection includes paintings, sculptures, prints, drawings, and photographs of prominent American statesmen, artists, writers, scientists, Native Americans, and explorers.

National Zoo

3001 Connecticut Avenue NW
Washington DC 20008
www.nationalzoo.si.edu
202.633.2614
Metrorail Red line (Woodley Park/Zoo/Adams Morgan, or Cleveland Park)

It's an awesome zoo!
NICOLE, AGE 9

The 163-acre National Zoo has long been acclaimed as one of the best and most attractive facilities of its kind in the country. Particularly impressive are the Komodo dragons, and the giant pandas from China, best seen at the 11 a.m. and 3 p.m. feeding times. The feeding and waking times for animals vary according to the season, so refer to an Information Station for a listing of the day's events. The Wetlands Exhibit around the Birdhouse and the prairie dogs across from the outdoor giraffe yard are treats for younger children. Other favorites include lions, tigers, and elephants. Older children and teens will enjoy learning about intelligence in the new Think Tank exhibit, while everyone marvels at orangutans crossing overhead on the O-Line between the Great Ape House and Think Tank.

The Navy Museum

736 Sicard Street SE
Washington DC 20374
www.history.navy.mil/branches/org8-1.htm
202.433.4882
Metrorail Blue, Green and Orange lines (Eastern Market or Navy Yard)

Permanent exhibits are devoted to the U.S. Navy from the underdog naval forces of the young United States in the Revolutionary War, through the polar explorations of Admiral Richard Byrd and Finn Ronne, to the Navy's role in the Korean War. Check out the simulated submarine combat center where visitors learn about the fundamentals of submarine technology through interactive displays. The submarine room also traces the development and history of the American submarine from Turtle to the Los Angeles class.

Newseum

555 Pennsylvania Avenue NW
Washington DC 20001
www.newseum.org
202.292.6100
Metrorail Green and Yellow lines (Archives)

This 250,000-square-foot news museum offers visitors a state-of-the-art experience that blends news history with up-to-the-second technology and hands-on exhibits. This interactive museum has seven-levels, fifteen theaters and fourteen galleries.

The Octagon

1799 New York Avenue NW
Washington DC 20006
www.theoctagon.org
202.626.7439
Metrorail Blue and Orange lines (Foggy Bottom)

The Octagon was built by Colonel John Tayloe III in 1800 to serve as his winter townhouse. During the War of 1812, the building served as the temporary White House for President and Mrs. Madison, and the Treaty of Ghent was signed here on February 17, 1815, ending that war. The Octagon served as the headquarters for the American Institute of Architects between 1889 and 1949 and is currently owned by the American Architectural Foundation. Trained docents discuss the early history of Washington, DC, the Tayloe family, the architecture of the house, and its decorative arts furnishings, and regale visitors with ghost stories. There are changing architectural exhibitions in the second floor galleries.

Old Post Office Tower

1100 Pennsylvania Avenue NW
Washington DC 20004
www.nps.gov/opot/index.htm
202.289.4225
Metrorail Blue, Orange and Red lines (Metro Center or Federal Triangle)
(AT TIME OF PRINTING CLOSED UNTIL 2016)

The Old Post Office was last restored and rededicated in 1983. Take a free tour of the 315-foot tall clock tower, which offers a breathtaking view of Washington from the 270-foot observation deck, and is home to the bells of the U.S. Congress.

Old Stone House

3051 M Street NW
Washington DC 20007
www.nps.gov/nr/travel/wash/dc17.htm
202.426.6851
Metrorail Blue and Orange lines (Foggy Bottom)

The Old Stone House is the oldest and only surviving pre-Revolutionary building in Washington. This was the modest home and shop of a Colonial cabinet-maker and is representative of a middle-class dwelling of the period. Its small size makes it seem cozy and comfortable to children. Older children may be intrigued by the rumors of a resident ghost.

The Phillips Collection

1600 21st Street NW
Washington DC 20009
www.phillipscollection.org
202.387.2151
Metrorail Red line (Dupont Circle)

The Phillips Collection, America's first museum of modern art, is a lovely and comfortable place to introduce children to art. This outstanding collection of mainly 19th- and 20th-century European and American painting and sculpture, with a sprinkling of old masters, is tastefully displayed in the former home of the Phillips family. Youngsters like the small rooms and connecting passageways that create a less formal atmosphere than a big museum, and with chairs in each room, children have a place to rest. Try to plan your visit around one of the family tours sometimes available for special exhibits. Don't miss Renoir's "Luncheon of the Boating Party" or other fine paintings by such artists as Bonnard, Braque, Daumier, Cezanne, or Klee.

Renwick Gallery

1661 Pennsylvania Avenue NW
Washington DC 20006
www.americanart.si.edu/renwick
202.633.7970
Metrorail Blue, Orange and Red lines (Farragut North and West)
(AT TIME OF PUBLICATION CLOSED FOR RENOVATIONS)

Designed in 1859 by architect James Renwick, Jr. to house the collection of William Corcoran, this building was Washington's first private art museum. Due to the growth in his collection, Corcoran moved his paintings and sculpture to the Corcoran Gallery of Art, and the Renwick became a showcase for contemporary American crafts. The Highlight Tour gives a general overview of the whole gallery, including the history of its two period rooms, the Grand Salon and the Octagon Room, and a quick showing of the current exhibits.

Smithsonian Art Museum

8th and F Streets NW
Washington DC 20004
www.americanart.si.edu
202.633.1000
Metrorail Green, Red and Yellow lines (Gallery Pl.–Chinatown)

Formerly the National Museum of American Art, the Smithsonian Art Museum is dedicated to American crafts from the 19th century to the present. Approximately 7,000 American artists are represented in the collection, including John Singer Sargent, Winslow Homer, Mary Cassatt, Georgia O'Keeffe, and Jacob Lawrence.

Textile Museum

701 21st Street NW
Washington DC 20052
www.museum.gwu.edu
202.994.5200
Metrorail Red line (Dupont Circle)
(AT TIME OF PUBLICATION IN PROCESS OF MOVING, TO REOPEN AT
NEW LOCATION SCHEDULED FOR LATE 2014)

The Textile Museum is devoted exclusively to the handmade
textile arts with a collection of over 17,000 rugs and textiles.
The Museum presents several changing exhibitions each year
which range from Oriental carpets to contemporary fiber art,
giving visitors a unique sampling of the richness and diversity
of the textile arts. Of special interest to children is the "Textile
Learning Center," comprised of two galleries: The Activity
Gallery and the Collections Gallery. The Activity Gallery is a
hands-on exhibition where visitors can learn about spinning,
dyeing, weaving, and other textiles. The Collections Gallery is
devoted to three rotating themes: How are Textiles Made? Who
Makes Textiles? and Why are Textiles Important?

Tudor Place

1644 31st Street NW
Washington DC 20007
www.tudorplace.org
202.965.0400
Metrorail Blue and Orange lines (Foggy Bottom)

Located in the heart of Georgetown on five fragrant landscaped
acres, Tudor Place was built for Martha Custis Peter,
granddaughter of Martha and George Washington. Purchased
for $8,000 and designed by Dr. William Thornton, architect
of the U.S. Capitol, Tudor Place remained in the Peter family
for 180 years. The household objects, sculpture, manuscripts,
etc. provide insight into America's history and culture in a
setting once frequented by Henry Clay, Daniel Webster, John
C. Calhoun, and General Robert E. Lee. A children's "look and
find" pamphlet helps focus young visitors' attention.

U.S. Holocaust Memorial Museum

100 15th Street NW
Washington DC 20024
www.ushmm.org
202.488.0400
Metrorail Blue and Orange lines (Smithsonian)

The Holocaust Museum is one of the most popular and talked about museums in Washington. People are drawn from all over the world to learn the history of the Holocaust and to try to understand the deeper meaning of this global tragedy. From the top floor of the building, visitors guide themselves down through each of four levels and are able to track the progression of the war, from Hitler's rise to power to the liberation of the camps following the German defeat. Interspersed within the historical time line are many opportunities to read, watch, and hear personal accounts of individuals who experienced the Holocaust.

U.S. Navy Memorial and Naval Heritage Center

701 Pennsylvania Avenue NW
Washington DC 20004
www.navymemorial.org
202.737.2300
Metrorail Green and Yellow lines (Archives)

The Navy Memorial includes both a commemorative public plaza and a Naval Heritage Center. The plaza is a round ceremonial amphitheater paved in granite to form a 100-foot diameter of the world. Surrounding the deck of the plaza are fountains, pools, flagpole masts, and sculptural panels depicting historic achievements of the sea services. A symbolic statue of a Lone Sailor stands watch near the edge of the plaza.

Union Station

50 Massachusetts Avenue NE
Washington DC 20002
www.unionstationdc.com
202.289.1908
Metrorail Red line (Union Station)

Just minutes from the Capital, Union Station contains over 125 stores, an immense food court, and a nine-screen movie complex. The restored 1907 Beaux-Arts structure—once the largest train station in the world—still serves as Washington's primary train station. Its classic lines in white granite set the stage for many of the early 20th century buildings and monuments of Washington—including the Lincoln and Jefferson Memorials and the Supreme Court building.

Washington National Cathedral

3101 Wisconsin Avenue NW
Washington DC 20016
www.nationalcathedral.org
202.537.6200
Metrorail Red line (Tenleytown, Dupont Circle, or Woodley Park)

This splendid Episcopal 14th-century style Gothic cathedral, started in 1907 and completed in 1990, is the sixth largest in the world. The tour of the main cathedral, small chapels, and crypts is especially interesting. The Children's Chapel impresses children with the stained glass, stonework, and other cathedral-related crafts. A visit to the Pilgrim Observation Gallery is also exciting, beginning with an elevator ride to the enclosed gallery at the roof level of the cathedral. The gallery affords an excellent view of Washington as well as the gargoyles, flying buttresses, and gardens of the cathedral. Don't miss the gardens and the herb cottage.

Washington Navy Yard and Art Gallery

Washington Navy Yard SE (Bldg. 76 for Gallery)
Washington DC 20374
www.history.navy.mil/branches/nhcorg6.htm
202.433.3815
Metrorail Green line (Navy Yard)

The Washington Navy Yard is the Navy's oldest shore establishment, home to the Naval Historical Center, which is comprised of the Navy Museum, Navy Art Gallery, and the display ship Barry, a decommissioned destroyer open to the public for self-guided tours.

Woodrow Wilson House

2340 S Street NW
Washington DC 20008
www.woodrowwilsonhouse.org
202.387.4062
Metrorail Red line (Dupont Circle)

Immediately following the inauguration ceremonies for
President Harding, Woodrow Wilson and his wife moved from
the White House to this stately town home and lived there until
his death. The only former President's house open to the public
in Washington, it still reflects the presence of this scholarly and
idealistic man. The drawing room and library have souvenirs
from all over the world. Children might also be interested in the
well-stocked kitchen of the 1920s, the 1915 elevator, and the
graphoscope, an early film projector.

Main Sights in Maryland

African Art Museum of Maryland

11711 East Market Place
Fulton MD 20759
www.africanartmuseum.org
301.490.6070

This museum displays African art and offers hands-on art experiences for children. Videos and slide shows enhance the exhibits.

Beall-Dawson House and Stonestreet Museum of 19th Century Medicine

103 W Montgomery Avenue
Rockville MD 20850
www.montgomeryhistory.org
301.762.1492

This 19th-century home teaches children of all ages about the history of Montgomery County. Tour guides make the tour fascinating to young visitors by pointing out some clues about rural life in the 19th century. The Stonestreet Museum of 19th Century Medicine is located on the grounds of the Beall-Dawson House. It is the original one-room office used by Dr. Edward Elijah Stonestreet from 1852-1903. This unique museum displays exhibits of medical, surgical, dental, and apothecary equipment. Children are delighted by the real skeleton, the Civil War amputation kit, and bleeding instruments. A hands-on reproduction of an 1850's stethoscope shows how difficult it was for a 19th century doctors to diagnose illnesses.

Belair Mansion

12207 Tulip Grove Drive
Bowie MD 20715
www.cityofbowie.org/index.aspx?NID=288
301.575.2488

The Belair Mansion, a Georgian plantation house built in about 1745 by the provincial governor of Maryland, Samuel Ogle, is filled with 18th century paintings, furniture, and silver.

Belair Stable

2835 Belair Drive
Bowie MD 20715
www.cityofbowie.org/index.aspx?NID=289
301.809.3089

The Belair Stable was built in 1907 and produced some of the greatest American thoroughbred racehorses. A small museum is on the grounds of the beautiful Belair Mansion. Groups of children can tour the estate with a docent and imagine what life might have been like on an 18th-century tobacco farm.

Bowie Train Station and Huntington Museum

8614 Chestnut Avenue
Bowie MD 20715
bowie.patch.com/listings/bowie-train-station-museum
301.805.4616

Children will particularly enjoy the railroad museum located at the site of the junction of the old Baltimore and Potomac Railroads founded in 1872. They can climb the tower at the depot and get a bird's eye view of trains as they fly by the station. Inside, they can send an imaginary message via telegraph and get an idea of communication in the pre-e-mail era.

Boyds Historical Society

19510 White Ground Road
Boyds MD 20841
www.boydshistory.org
301.461.4646

The primary attraction is the Boyds Negro School. This one-room 22 x 30 foot wooden building, heated by a wood stove, served as the only public school for African Americans in the

Boyds area from 1895-1936. The schoolhouse served students in grades 1-8, many of whom walked for miles to attend classes at the school. After the purchase of the property in 1980, the school was restored by Boyds Historical Society to its original condition in approximately 1900.

Clara Barton National Historic Site

5801 Oxford Road
Glen Echo MD 20812
www.nps.gov/clba/index.htm
301.320.1410

Visit the home of Clara Barton, who founded the American Red Cross in 1881. This house was not only her home from 1897-1912, but also the headquarters of the American Red Cross from 1897-1904. The Clara Barton National Historic Site, established in 1975 to commemorate both Miss Barton and the early American Red Cross, offers educational tours for children (grades K-6) stressing the role volunteers played.

College Park Aviation Museum

1985 Corporal Frank Scott Drive
College Park MD 20740
www.collegeparkaviationmuseum.com
301.864.6029
Metrorail Green and Yellow line (College Park)

The College Park Airport was founded in 1909 by the Wright Brothers and is the oldest continuously operating airport in the world. It serves as the general aviation airport for small privately-owned aircraft and is the site of many famous "firsts" including the first U.S. Army flying school and the first commercial airmail service. The College Park Aviation Museum commemorates the historic importance of the airport. This interactive, hands-on museum has exhibits and year-round programs including an animatronic Wilbur Wright, vintage aircraft, and museum-quality replicas of early airplanes. Family-oriented programs include model-making and kite-building workshops, lectures, film series, and children's events.

The Dennis and Philip Ratner Museum

10001 Old Georgetown Road
Bethesda MD 20814
www.ratnermuseum.org
301.897.1518

The Dennis and Phillip Ratner Museum was established "to foster love of the Bible through the graphic arts." The museum's three buildings include a Resource Center, including library, conference space, and children's art and literature museum. The Resource Center contains an Ark, Eternal Light, Menorah, and Torah.

Glen Echo Park and Carousel

7300 MacArthur Boulevard
Glen Echo MD 20812
www.glenechopark.org
301.634.2222

Glen Echo Park was originally the site of a National Chataqua Assembly, and later a well-known amusement park. The National Park Service has converted this former amusement park into an arts center with over 500 art classes per year, covering the visual and performing arts. The park houses a number of artists-in-residence who are often available to discuss their work with the public. It is also home to Adventure Theater (see page 111) and the Puppet Company Playhouse (see page 121), which offer family performances. In addition be sure to make some time to ride the famous Carousel. Glen Echo offers many classes and summer camps.

Good Knight Kingdom Museum

11001 Rhode Island Avenue
Beltsville MD 20705
www.goodknight.org/castle_contact.html
301.595.8989

The Good Knight Kingdom features displays and activities that teach children and parents about child safety in an entertaining way. Exhibits cover basic safety tips on fire, poison, and household safety, as well as more serious topics such as drug and alcohol abuse, molestation, and abduction. Through the exhibits, children learn to face these modern "dragons" and receive a Certificate of Knighthood when they complete the sessions.

Greenbelt Museum

10B Crescent Road
Greenbelt MD 20770
www.greenbeltmuseum.org
301.507.6582

Greenbelt is one of three "green towns" built by the federal government in an effort to provide jobs during the Great Depression. As one of America's earliest and most successful planned towns, Greenbelt is a National Historic Landmark. The Greenbelt Museum is located in an original home, half of a duplex building, built by the federal government. The home appears much as it did in 1937 when the first residents were selected by the government to move into the town of the future. The collection includes early photographs of the town, Art Deco pieces, and furniture. The home is adjacent to many of the revolutionary planning features of the town: inner walkways, a pedestrian underpass, and a town center.

John Poole House

19923 Fisher Avenue
Poolesville MD 20837
www.historicmedley.org/visit/john-poole-house
301.972.8588

The oldest building in Poolesville, this log house was built in 1793 by John Poole Junior as a trading post for merchants and families of surrounding farms and plantations. It also served as a post office and was a stimulus to growth in the area. One room contains Civil War artifacts and an adjoining small arboretum displays plants native to the area before 1850.

Marietta House Museum

5626 Bell Station Road
Glenn Dale MD 20769
history.pgparks.com/sites_and_museums/Marietta_House_Museum.htm
301.464.5654

Gabriel Duvall, a Justice of the U.S. Supreme Court, built this Federal-style country home between 1812 and 1813. The home is the current headquarters of the Prince George's County Historical Society and the Society's library. The house is furnished according to four periods of the 19th century.

The land surrounding Marietta was a working farm where the Duvall family raised tobacco and grain crops. Walk around the grounds to see a root cellar, the Judge's law office, and a cemetery with family gravestones.

Montpelier Mansion

9650 Muirkirk Road
Laurel MD 20708
www.pgelegantsettings.com/Our_Sites/Montpelier_Mansion.htm
301.377.7817

Completed in the 1780s, Montpelier is a masterpiece of Georgian architecture. The expansive grounds (75 acres) include a boxwood maze and one of the two remaining 18th-century gazebos in the nation that is still on its original site. The property is atop a high bluff overlooking the Patuxent River, one of the most beautiful views in the state. Children enjoy seeing the Quaker classrooms and secret staircase. The Montpelier Cultural Arts Center is located in a modern barn on the property. It is open seven days a week from 10-5 (except holidays). The Arts Center features artists in residence, art galleries, and classes. Exhibits range from paintings to pottery.

Montgomery County Airpark

7940 Airpark Road
Gaithersburg MD 20879
www.montgomerycountyairpark.com
301.963.8043

Montgomery County Airpark is Maryland's fourth busiest airport. Visitors can see piston and jet aircraft land, eat at the on-site restaurant with a view of the runway, or take an airplane or helicopter ride. There is a grassy area for picnics. Free group tours are given by appointment.

NASA/Goddard Space Flight Center

8800 Greenbelt Road
Greenbelt MD 20771
www.nasa.gov/centers/goddard/home/index.html
301.286.2000

NASA's Goddard Space Flight Center presents exhibits that highlight the space program's contribution to communications, navigation, and aeronautics. School children of all ages will find something to fascinate them. Real and model rockets and satellites are on exhibit both outside and inside. Dock the Manned-Maneuvering Unit Simulator with a satellite by manipulating the controls. Use the computer system to build your own satellite and rocket system. The computer will alert you to any mistakes. Sunspots and solar flares can be witnessed as they happen with the solar telescope. Watch as weather maps of the earth are transmitted here from space. View recent footage of NASA's space ventures on a giant TV.

National Capital Trolley Museum

1313 Bonifant Road
Colesville MD 20905
www.dctrolley.org
301.384.6088

The highlight of this small museum is a 20-minute ride on an old-time trolley through the surrounding woods; the staff relates history and anecdotes about the cars. Try to schedule your visit for one of the occasional open houses held throughout the year; all five trolleys run and you can choose to ride on the German, Austrian, or DC cars. On regular weekends, only one trolley runs at a time.

National Children's Museum

151 St George Boulevard
National Harbor MD 20745
www.ccm.org
301.392.2400

Designed primarily for children age 8 and younger, the National Children's Museum (NCM) is a nationally recognized cultural and educational institution serving children and families onsite and through national partners and programs. The Museum's exhibits and innovative educational programs spark the imagination and celebrate the true power of children, motivating them to become people who make a difference in the world.

National Cryptologic Museum and National Vigilance Park

8290 Colony Seven Road
Annapolis Junction MD 20701
www.nsa.gov/about/cryptologic_heritage/museum/index.shtml
301.688.5849

The National Cryptologic Museum, created by the National Security Agency, is the first and only public museum in the U.S. government intelligence community. Exhibits examine the breaking of the Enigma codes and a look at the Navajo Code Talkers, along with other dramatic historical moments in American code making and code breaking, and machines, devices, and techniques employed by dense cryptologists. The adjacent National Vigilance Park showcases two reconnaissance aircraft used for secret missions.

National Harbor

www.nationalharbor.com

National Harbor is a 300-acre multi-use waterfront development on the shores of the Potomac River in Prince George's County, Maryland just south of Washington, DC near the Woodrow Wilson Bridge. You can also visit National Harbor by boat from Alexandria!

National Museum of Health and Medicine of the Armed Forces

2500 Linden Lane
Silver Spring MD 20910
www.medicalmuseum.mil
301.319.3300
Metrorail Red line (Silver Spring and Forest Glen)

Originally established during the Civil War as the Army Medical Museum, this is one of the few places where you can learn about medical history, the human body, and disease by actually seeing real specimens. Some are graphic and may not be appropriate for all ages or for those who are squeamish. The permanent collection is divided into: Historical, Anatomical, Neuroanatomical, and the Human Developmental Anatomy Section.

Radio and Television Museum

2608 Mitchellville Road
Bowie MD 20716
www.ncrtv.org
301.390.1020

Enter the 1906 Harmel house country store and explore the history of radio. Learn about the history of radio from Marconi's earliest wireless telegraph to the primitive crystal sets of the 1920s, through Depression-era cathedrals and the post-War plastic portable radios, and, finally, to the development of radio with pictures, called televisions.

The Sandy Spring Museum

17901 Bentley Road
Sandy Spring MD 20860
www.sandyspringmuseum.org
301.774.0022

Sandy Spring Museum is a non-profit community museum, established in 1980, whose mission is to bring local history to life by "time traveling" to the era of our founding fathers and exploring the world of the early settlers at work, play, school, and home. Their story is brought vividly to life with a rich assortment of artifacts, visual images, hands-on objects, and oral presentations. The museum's on-site and outreach programs are designed to complement classroom lessons in social studies. The museum has a collection of old-fashioned toys that children may play with during or after the tour.

SPAGnVOLA Chocolate Factory Tour

360 Main Street
Gaithersburg MD 20878
www.spagnvola.com/pages/factory-tours
240.654.6972

SPAGnVOLA offers free factory tours every weekend which you can sign up for on their website. SPAGnVOLA cultivates and processes their own cacao beans from their estate in the Dominican Republic. Once in the Gaithersburg store, the beans are roasted and refined in small batches to bring out the flavor. There is a large variety of finished products to take home after your tour.

Surratt House Museum

9118 Brandywine Road
Clinton MD 20735
history.pgparks.com/sites_and_museums/Surratt_House_Museum.htm
301.868.1121

This two-story frame house was a tavern, post office, polling place and home of the first woman executed by the U.S. government, Mary Surratt. In July 1865, she was hung for her alleged role in the assassination of President Abraham Lincoln. John Wilkes Booth stopped briefly at the house the evening of April 14, 1865, as he tried to escape after shooting the President. Today, costumed docents give visitors tours of the home and discuss the question of whether or not Mary Surratt was a co-conspirator in the assassination plot. The home is a typical middle class home of the Victorian period. The displays include Victorian furniture, rugs, lace curtains, clothing and kitchen implements.

Uncle Tom's Cabin (Riley House/Josiah Henson's Cabin)

11420 Old Georgetown Road
Rockville MD 20852
www.montgomeryparks.org/PPSD/Cultural_Resources_Stewardship/
heritage/josiahhensonsp.shtm
301.650.4373

This 13-by-17-foot 18th-century cabin is the former home of slave Josiah Henson, whose autobiography *The Life of Josiah Henson, Formerly a Slave* was the model for Harriet Beecher Stowe's novel *Uncle Tom's Cabin*. Josiah Henson was born in 1789 in Charles County, Maryland. Before he escaped to Canada on the Underground Railroad, Henson was sold to, worked and lived on the Montgomery County plantation owned by Isaac Riley.

Washington Temple Visitors' Center ("Mormon Temple")

9900 Stoneybrook Drive
Kensington MD 20895
www.lds.org/locations/washington-dc-temple-visitors-center
301.587.0144

The Washington, DC Mormon Temple, dedicated in 1974, is the largest in the United States. It is an extraordinary edifice covered in 173,000 feet of white marble, and situated on 57 acres in Kensington, Maryland. The International Visitors Center is open to the public, and offers films and exhibits describing the temple's construction, and programs of the church. Be sure to visit during the holiday season for their famous Christmas lights!

White's Ferry

24801 Whites Ferry Road
Dickerson MD 20842
canal.mcmullans.org/whites_ferry.htm
301.349.5200

A 15-car ferry crosses the Potomac River to connect with Route 15, two miles from Leesburg on the Virginia side. The ferry is the only cable-guided fresh water ferry on the east coast, and is the last operating ferry across the Potomac River. The fishing is reputedly good in the area because a Pepco plant upstream in Dickerson warms the river. For a minimum of four people, you (and canoe) are taken to Point-of-Rocks, about ten miles upstream. Depending on weather conditions, the trip downstream will take about six hours, during which you can fish, float, or socialize. You might also plan a hike on the C&O Canal.

Main Sights in Virginia

Alexandria Archaeology Museum

105 N Union Street
Alexandria VA 22314
www.alexandriava.gov/Archaeology
703.746.4399
Metrorail Yellow line (King Street)

The Alexandria Archaeology Museum was formed to preserve and interpret archaeological information from the diverse city of Alexandria and to involve the public in archaeological preservation. At the museum's lab, children can observe volunteers working with artifacts, cleaning, and cataloging. Visitors also see a life-size model of an archaeologist at work. The organization encourages participation in field trips to archaeological digs when possible.

Alexandria Black History Resource Center

902 Wythe Street
Alexandria VA 22314
www.alexandriava.gov/BlackHistory
703.746.4356
Metrorail Blue and Yellow lines (King Street or Braddock Street)

The mission of the Black History Museum is to enrich the lives of Alexandria's residents and visitors, to foster tolerance and understanding among all cultures and to stimulate appreciation of the diversity of the African American experience. The institutional complex is composed of the Museum, the Watson Reading Room, and the Alexandria African American Heritage Park.

Arlington House/The Robert E. Lee Memorial

1 Memorial Drive
Arlington VA 22202
www.nps.gov/arho
703.235.1530
Metrorail Blue line (Arlington Cemetery)

Robert E. Lee courted and wed Mary Custis in this hilltop
mansion. They lived here for 30 years, from 1831-1861, and
raised seven children here. It has been restored with some of
the original furnishings and similar pieces of the 1850s. Don't
miss the magnificent view of the Washington skyline from the
front portico, which Lafayette described as the "finest view in
the world." Show the children the upstairs children's room and
playroom. The house is staffed by park rangers.

Arlington National Cemetery

1 Memorial Drive
Arlington VA 22202
www.arlingtoncemetery.mil
877.907.8585
Metrorail Blue line (Arlington Cemetery)

To bring the subject of war down to a comprehensible level
for both children and adults, there is no better place than
the Arlington National Cemetery. The sheer expanse of the
cemetery, 612 acres, with its vast number of graves spanning
the time period from the American Revolution to the present,
brings a sense of the finality and devastation of our wars. At the
Information Center, one can obtain the location of the burial
site for any individual buried here. In addition to soldiers'
graves, sections of the cemetery are dedicated to veterans who
were astronauts, chaplains, and nurses. And be sure to take the
time to visit the famous Tomb of the Unknown Soldier.

Carlyle House Historic Park

121 N Fairfax Street
Alexandria VA 22314
www.nvrpa.org/park/carlyle_house_historic_park
703.549.2997
Metrorail Blue and Yellow lines (King Street or Braddock Street)

This English, country-style mansion was built by Scottish
merchant John Carlyle in 1753. The home was a social and

political center and the site of a historic governor's conference at the outset of the French and Indian War. The Carlyle House is on the National Register of Historic Places and is Alexandria's only stone, 18th-century Palladian-style house.

Christ Church

118 North Washington Street
Alexandria VA 22314
www.historicchristchurch.org
703.549.1450

This lovely colonial Georgian church, in continual use since its completion in 1773, is the oldest in Alexandria and one of the oldest on the East Coast. Visitors can sit in the boxed-in pew belonging to George Washington. Look for the little brass tablet that marks where Robert E. Lee knelt at the altar rail to be confirmed. Franklin Roosevelt and Winston Churchill attended services on the World Day of Prayer for Peace, January 1, 1942.

Colvin Run Mill Historic Site

10017 Colvin Run Road
Great Falls VA 22066
www.fairfaxcounty.gov/parks/colvinrunmill
703.759.2771

Colvin Run Mill, built in the early 1800s, is a working grist-mill that produces whole grain products to sell in the on-site general store. The huge grinding stones, the wooden gears, and the outside water wheel fascinates children of all ages.

Drug Enforcement Administration Museum and Visitors Center

700 Army Navy Drive
Arlington VA 22202
www.deamuseum.org
202.307.3463
Metrorail Blue and Yellow lines (Pentagon City)

This provocative museum intended for teens and adults attempts to show the stark realities of drug use in America. Drug paraphernalia and grisly photos are displayed along with a history of intoxication and drug use over the course of the last century, along with a look at the historical, global influences of drug trafficking from the ancient Silk Road to the present.

Fort Ward Museum and Historic Site

4301 W Braddock Road
Alexandria VA 22304
www.alexandriava.gov/fortward
703.746.4848

Of special interest to Civil War buffs, this museum exhibits
weapons, uniforms, musical instruments, and other memorabilia
of the period. Children can learn about the everyday life of Civil
War soldiers and civilians. In addition to the museum building,
there is a Civil War fort, and an Officers' Hut located within the
adjacent Fort Ward Park.

Friendship Firehouse

107 S Alfred Street
Alexandria VA 22314
www.alexandriava.gov/friendshipfirehouse
703.746.3891

The Friendship Fire Company was established in 1774 and was
the first volunteer fire company in Alexandria. The company
moved to this house in the 1850's. The first floor Engine Room
features hand drawn fire engines, buckets, axes, hoses, and
other historic firefighting apparatus, along with reproduction
equipment that children can handle.

Gadsby's Tavern Museum

134 N Royal Street
Alexandria VA 22314
www.alexandriava.gov/gadsbystavern
703.746.4242

Gadsby's Tavern Museum offers an exciting look into the
operations of an 18th-century tavern. The Museum consists
of the 1770 City Tavern and the 1792 City Hotel, named after
John Gadsby, the Englishman who operated them between 1796
and 1808. The tour covers architectural highlights, a display of
period objects and furnishings, and the ballroom where George
Washington danced to celebrate his birthday in 1798 and 1799.

George Washington Masonic National Memorial

101 Callahan Drive
Alexandria VA 22301
www.gwmemorial.org
703.683.2007
Metrorail Blue and Yellow lines (King Street)

This memorial to George Washington towers over the Alexandria skyline, affording a good view of the area. Memorabilia displayed include George Washington's Bible, a clock that was stopped at the time of his death, and other Washington artifacts. Children enjoy the animatronic George Washington and the large mechanical model of a Shriner's parade, complete with platoons of brightly clad nobles marching to recorded band music.

Gunston Hall Plantation

10709 Gunston Road
Mason Neck VA 22079
www.gunstonhall.org
703.550.9220

This Colonial plantation is one of the finest homes in the area, with its tasteful interior and spacious grounds overlooking the Potomac River. Gunston Hall was the home of George Mason, an author of Virginia's Declaration of Rights. The 18th-century furnishings and the intricately carved woodwork are outstanding. The children's rooms and nursery contain simple, small-scale furniture of the period. A museum features mementos from the Mason family, and a diorama shows how the plantation worked. Outbuildings include the kitchen, dairy, smokehouse, schoolhouse, and laundry. The formal gardens contain boxwood hedges.

Iwo Jima Memorial

On the George Washington Parkway
Arlington VA 22209
www.nps.gov/gwmp/historyculture/usmcwarmemorial.htm
703.289.2500

The United States Marine Corps War Memorial stands as a symbol of this grateful Nation's esteem for the honored dead of the U.S. Marine Corps. The statue depicts one of the most famous incidents of World War II, the raising of the American flag on Mt. Suribachi in February 1945. The photographer Joe Rosenthal won a Pulitzer Prize for his photograph of the flag raising, and sculptor Felix W. deWeldon captured that image in the bronze sculpture at the memorial. The memorial is dedicated to all Marines who have given their lives in the defense of the Unites States since 1775.

The Lee-Fendall House Museum

614 Oronoco Street
Alexandria VA 22314
www.leefendallhouse.org
703.548.1789

Built in 1785 by Robert E. Lee's uncle, Philip Fendall, and steeped in Civil War history, this house has been restored to reflect its early Victorian period. This child-friendly house offers hands-on items and specialized educational programs. Advance reservations are recommended.

The Lyceum, Alexandria's History Museum

201 S Washington Street
Alexandria VA 22314
www.alexandriava.gov/Lyceum
703.746.4994
Metrorail Blue and Yellow lines (King Street)

In 1985, The Lyceum became Alexandria's History Museum, providing exhibitions, school programs, lectures and concerts, volunteer opportunities and space for rental functions for the community. The Lyceum Museum Shop carries a wide variety of maps, books, note cards and special items related to Alexandria's history. The Lyceum offers a variety of programs for students, children, and families throughout the year. The programs can be tailored to meet the specific needs of your group.

Market Square/Alexandria City Hall

301 King Street
Alexandria VA 22314
www.alexandriava.gov/FarmersMarket
703.746.4994

During the original survey of Alexandria in 1749, two half-acre lots were set aside for a market place and town hall. In the course of the town's history, this site has held schools, jails, whipping posts, and a town courthouse. On Saturday mornings, it is the home of one of the oldest continuously operating markets in the country.

Morven Park

17263 Southern Planter Lane
Leesburg VA 20176
www.morvenpark.org
703.777.6034

This 1,200-acre estate is operated as a memorial to Westmoreland Davis, former Governor of Virginia. Children tend to be most interested in the extensive vehicle collection. In the old carriage house and Carriage Museum, there are coaches, breaks, and gigs driven by turn-of-the-century American society members, plus everyday phaetons, surreys, carts, sleighs, a funeral hearse, and a charcoal-burning fire engine.

Mount Vernon Estate and Gardens (George Washington's Home)

3200 Mt Vernon Memorial Highway
Mount Vernon VA 22121
www.mountvernon.org
703.780.2000

This elegant and stately plantation mansion was the home of George Washington. Guests visiting the estate can view Washington's Mansion and many other original structures. The historic footprint also includes the tomb of George and Martha Washington and a memorial dedicated to the enslaved people who lived and worked on the estate. Interpretive spaces such as the Pioneer Farm and George Washington's Gristmill & Distillery provide a rich understanding of Washington's enterprising and profitable business ventures.

National Firearms Museum

11250 Waples Mill Road
Fairfax VA 22030
www.nramuseum.org
703.267.1620
Metrorail Orange line (Vienna)

The NRA (National Rifle Association) has a collection of 3,500 historically significant firearms from 1450 to the present day.

Oatlands Plantation

20850 Oatlands Plantation Lane
Leesburg VA 20175
www.oatlands.org
703.777.3174

This hunt-country estate dates from the early 1800s. Decorative and unusual features, such as the octagonal drawing room and a flanking pair of staircases, make for a worthwhile visit, especially for those interested in architecture. There is a terraced, four-acre, formal English garden, considered one of the finest examples of early Virginia landscape design, a tea house, and a reflecting pool.

Stabler-Leadbeater Apothecary Shop and Museum

107 S Fairfax Street
Alexandria VA 22314
www.alexandriava.gov/Apothecary
703.746.3852
Metrorail Blue and Yellow lines (King Street and Braddock Street)

George Washington, Robert E. Lee, Daniel Webster, and other historical figures used this actual drugstore. Original prescription books and a sampling of pharmaceutical equipment are on display. A recording relates the shop's history.

Steven F. Udvar-Hazy Air and Space Center

14390 Air and Space Museum Parkway
Chantilly VA 20151
www.airandspace.si.edu/visit/udvar-hazy-center
703.572.4118

The Steven F. Udvar-Hazy Center near Dulles Airport is the companion facility to the Air and Space Museum on the National Mall. The Udvar-Hazy center is comprised of two display areas, the Boeing Aviation Hangar and the James S. McDonnell Space Hangar, the Donald D. Engen Observation Tower, an IMAX Theater, space simulators, museum store and kiosks, a café offering basic fare and multimedia classrooms/learning labs. Highlights of the museum include the Lockheed SR-71 Blackbird, the fastest jet in the world, some of the tiniest aircraft in the world and the space shuttle Enterprise. On display in this exciting space are 141 aircraft, more than 145 large space artifacts and over 1,500 smaller items.

Sully Historic Site

3650 Historic Sully Way
Chantilly VA 20151
www.fairfaxcounty.gov/parks/sully
703.437.1794

Programs at the Sully Historic Site emphasize the enslaved African American community, and show what life was like throughout the 18th and 19th centuries. One of several restored Lee family houses in Virginia, Sully Historic Site was built in 1794 for Richard B. Lee, first Congressman of Northern Virginia and uncle of General Robert E. Lee.

Torpedo Factory Art Center

105 N Union Street
Alexandria VA 22314
www.torpedofactory.org
703.838.4565
Metrorail Yellow line (King Street)

Located on the Potomac riverfront in historic Old Town Alexandria, the Torpedo Factory Art Center has 83 studios and six galleries housing more than 165 artists and craftsmen working, exhibiting, and selling their art in this renovated World War I munitions plant. Families may explore the Factory on their own, and have lunch at one of the Old Town's many restaurants or the Food Court located behind the Art Center.

Woodlawn Plantation/Frank Lloyd Wright's Pope-Leighey House

9000 Richmond Highway
Alexandria VA 22309
www.woodlawnpopeleighey.org
703.780.4000

George Washington gave part of his Mount Vernon estate to his granddaughter, Nelly Custis, and his nephew, Lawrence Lewis, as a wedding present. Woodlawn Mansion, designed by Dr. William Thorton, architect of the U.S. Capitol, was built here. Adults will appreciate the elegant living room, dining room, and parlor. Youngsters like the children's bedrooms and the collection of stuffed birds acquired by Nelly Custis' son. A restored garden features roses and boxwood plantings. As a plantation site, Woodlawn was also home to over 90 slaves, as well as free hired workers, black and white.

The Great Outdoors

E xplore history by visiting battlefields and historic farms; learn about plants, animals and the night sky; get out and play: Washington has many open-air opportunities for fun and many ways to connect with the great outdoors. Before you plan your trip, be sure to call or check websites for hours and directions.

Anacostia Park

1900 Anacostia Drive SE
Washington DC 20020
www.nps.gov/anac
202.472.3884
Metrorail Green line (Anacostia)

This large area along the east bank of the Anacostia River has playing fields for football and baseball, picnic spots, playgrounds, basketball courts, an outdoor swimming pool, and an outdoor pavilion for roller-skating and community gatherings. One section of the park has been designated as a bird sanctuary, where you might see a variety of marshland birds such as herons, egrets, ducks, and geese. For a close-up view of plants and wildlife, bring your own canoe and paddle along the banks of the river and its inlets.

Battery-Kemble Park

49th Street NW and Garfield Street NW
Washington DC 20016
www.nps.gov/cwdw/historyculture/battery-kemble.htm
202.895.6070

Without leaving the city, you can enjoy an afternoon picnic and a nature walk in this fine, hilly, woodsy park. Historically a part of the circle of Civil War Defenses of Washington, DC, Battery-

Kemble is one of the best area locations for sledding and cross-country skiing, and is ideal for kite flying.

Capital Crescent Trail

Georgetown to Silver Spring (11 miles)
www.cctrail.org
202.234.4874

The Capital Crescent Trail is an approximately 11-mile long hiker/biker trail running from Silver Spring to Georgetown along the former B&O Railroad line. The trail crosses four historic bridges and runs through two historic tunnels and provides a look at the Potomac River through some of the prettiest woodlands in Washington. The trail connects with both the C&O towpath and with the Rock Creek Trail. The entrance to the trail in Bethesda is at the corner of Bethesda and Woodmont Avenues.

Glover-Archbold Park

Tenleytown to Georgetown
Washington DC 20050
www.mcleangardens.com/item_list.asp?subcat=167&subtitle=Glover
+Archbold+Park+and+Nature+Trail

Leave the hustle and bustle of the city behind as you enter this serene, heavily wooded park to wander its nature trails, bird watch, or day dream. This section of Rock Creek Park runs from MacArthur Boulevard and Canal Road, NW to just south of Van Ness Street and Wisconsin Avenue NW, between 42nd and 44th Streets NW. Look for community gardens, planted and tended by local residents, in the section of the park closest to Whitehaven Park.

Rock Creek Park

Rock Creek and Potomac Parkway
Washington DC 20008
www.nps.gov/rocr/index.htm
202.895.6000

Rock Creek is a wooded 1,754-acre park, about four miles long and one mile wide that runs through northwest Washington from the Potomac River into Montgomery County Maryland. Picnic groves with tables, fireplaces, and shelters are abundant.

A 1.5-mile exercise course begins near Calvert Street and Connecticut Avenue, NW, and another begins at 16th and Kennedy Streets, NW. The park's many resources include: The National Zoo (see page 29), Rock Creek Nature Center and Planetarium (see page 95), and the Rock Creek Gallery, site of children's activities and art exhibits. Call 202.244.2482 for information on the gallery programs.

IN MARYLAND

Black Hill Regional Park

20930 Lake Ridge Drive
Boyds MD 20841
www.montgomeryparks.org/facilities/regional_parks/blackhill
301.528.3490

This park is located on more than 200 acres, including Little Seneca Lake with 16 miles of shoreline. The two challenging playgrounds are favorites of younger children. There is also a picnic area (call to reserve shelters, 301.495.2480), a Visitor Center, a paved hiker/biker trail, ten miles of hiking and equestrian trails, horseshoe pits, volleyball courts, boat launching, canoe and rowboat rentals, and fishing.

Calvert Cliffs State Park

9500 H.G. Trueman Road
Lusby MD 20657
www.dnr.state.md.us/publiclands/southern/calvertcliffs.asp
301.743.7613

On the western side of the Chesapeake Bay, the Cliffs of Calvert dominate the shoreline for thirty miles along the shores of Calvert County. They are as impressive a sight today as they were when Captain John Smith came upon them in his exploration of the Bay in 1608. The cliffs were formed over fifteen million years ago when all of southern Maryland was covered by a warm shallow sea. These ancient sea floors can now be seen carved into the cliffs.

Catoctin Mountain Park

14707 Park Central Road
Thurmont MD 21788
www.nps.gov/cato/index.htm
301.663.9388

This park offers campsites, hiking trails, picnic tables and grills, and fishing streams (fly fishing allowed, catch and release only). In winter, when there may be up to twelve inches of snow, there is ample cross-country skiing, snow shoeing, and sledding. A variety of special events for children and adults, including campfire programs and nature walks, make this park a memorable retreat for the whole family. Group camps are also available.

Cedarville State Forest

10201 Bee Oak Road
Brandywine MD 20613
www.dnr.state.md.us/publiclands/southern/cedarville.asp
301.888.1410

This area was once the winter home of southern Maryland's Piscataway Indians, who lived near Zekiah Swamp, where wildlife was abundant and the weather was mild. There are plenty of picnic tables, shelters, and charcoal grills (no wood fire permitted). The park features 19.5 miles of marked trails for hiking, biking and horseback riding, a pond for fishing, nature walks, and campfire programs. In the summer, the Visitors Center at Maryland's only warm water fish hatchery is open to the public.

Chesapeake and Ohio (C&O) Canal

Historical Great Falls Park, MD
Potomac MD 20854
www.nps.gov/choh/index.htm
301.983.0825

With spectacular rock formations, the Great Falls portion of the C&O Canal is one of the most impressive natural sights in this area. Here the river drops more than seventy feet over numerous falls and proceeds downstream through rapids and river islands to its junction with the tidal estuary at Little Falls (Chain Bridge). The park consists of nine hundred acres on the Maryland side of the Potomac.

Cosca Regional Park

11000 Thrift Road
Clinton MD 20735
www.pgparks.com/Things_To_Do/Nature/Cosca_Regional_Park.htm
301.868.1397

With 690 acres including rolling and wooded terrain and a
15-acre lake, Cosca Regional Park offers a variety of recreation
for any outdoor enthusiast, and is home to the Clearwater Nature
Center (see page 91). The park features equestrian and hiking
trails, lighted athletic fields, indoor and outdoor tennis courts
(for schedule and fees for indoor courts, call 301.868.6462),
picnic grounds, and play areas. Campers have access to
bathhouses, toilet facilities, water hook-ups, and electricity.

Cunningham Falls State Park

14039 Catoctin Hollow Road
Thurmont MD 21788
www.dnr.state.md.us/publiclands/western/cunningham.asp
301.271.7574

Named for the splendid 78-foot waterfall that cascades in a
rocky gorge, the 4,446-acre park offers nature walks, campfire
programs, picnicking (tables, grills, and one shelter), and hiking.
The 43-acre lake offers boat launching, canoe rental, fishing,
and swimming. There are family campsites in both areas of the
park, and a playground made from 3000 tires at the Manor
area. In the winter, this is a great place for cross-country skiing
and sledding.

Dickerson Conservation Area

20700 Martinsburg Road
Dickerson MD 20842
www.montgomeryparks.org/parks_facilities_directory/dickersoncp.shtm

This 304-acre park is located along the Potomac River and the
C&O Canal just south of the boundary between Montgomery
and Frederick Counties on a portion of the C&O Canal and
towpath that was damaged during the flood of 1996. It is a
fisherman's dream spot as well as a great place to picnic or
stroll along the canal.

Greenbelt Park

6565 Greenbelt Road
Greenbelt MD 20770
www.nps.gov/gree/index.htm
301.344.3948

Greenbelt Park has 174 woodland campsites for tents, recreational vehicles, and trailers up to 30 feet long. Restrooms, picnic tables, fireplaces, showers, and water are available, but there are no utility hook-ups. There are several hiking trails and one large field for playing ball. The 1,100-acre woods have picnic areas and three nature trails. Park rangers lead campfire programs and nature walks in the summer, and offer a Junior Ranger Program for children.

Lake Artemesia Park

Berwyn Road & 55th Avenue
Berwyn Heights MD 20740
www.pgparks.com/page328.aspx
301.627.7755

Lake Artemesia is a 38-acre, man-made lake with over two miles of accessible hiker-biker trails. The lake is stocked with several varieties of fish (bass, bluegill, sunfish, catfish, and trout). Lake Artemesia is also part of the Anacostia Tributary Trail System that encompasses the northeast/northwest branches of the Anacostia River.

Lake Frank

6700 Needwood Road
Derwood MD 20855
www.montgomeryparks.org/facilities/regional_parks/rockcreek
301.948.5053

Lake Frank is part of Rock Creek Regional Park. Offering shoreline hiking and fishing, this is a rustic, quiet spot to "get away from it all."

Lake Needwood

6700 Needwood Road
Derwood MD 20855
www.montgomeryparks.org/facilities/regional_parks/rockcreek
301.948.5053

A picturesque man-made lake, well used for boating and fishing, Lake Needwood offers plenty of activities for a full day outdoors. You can take a trip aboard the "Needwood Queen," a 20-passenger pontoon boat, or rent a paddleboat, rowboat, or canoe. Lake Needwood is a good place to go fishing (you can purchase bait and a fishing license at the boat house). There are also hiking trails, play areas, picnic groves, a snack bar, and bathrooms. The Meadowside Nature Center is located here (see page 94).

Little Bennett Regional Park

23701 Frederick Road
Clarksburg MD 20871
www.montgomeryparks.org/facilities/regional_parks/little_bennett
301.528.3450

Take a short ride north of the busy Washington, DC area to a pleasant and secluded camping and hiking area in Little Bennett Regional Park. The family campground features picnic tables and grills, comfort stations (sinks, showers, and toilets), water spigots, horseshoes, volleyball, and activity programs on Saturdays (April-October). This is also an excellent place to go for a day hike. Pack a lunch and set out on one of the park's many trails. The remains of several sites of historic interest are located on these trails: saw mills, a 19th-century schoolhouse, and several houses. Fishing is available at nearby Little Seneca Lake.

Patapsco Valley State Park

8020 Baltimore National Pike
Ellicott City MD 21043
www.dnr.state.md.us/publiclands/central/patapsco.asp
410.461.5006

Patapsco Valley State Park extends along 32 miles of the Patapsco River, encompassing 16,043 acres and eight developed recreational areas. Recreational opportunities include hiking, fishing, camping, canoeing, horseback riding, and mountain bike trails, as well as picnicking for individuals or large groups in the park's many popular pavilions.

Piscataway National Park

13551 Fort Washington Road
Fort Washington, MD 20744
www.nps.gov/pisc/index.htm
301.763.4600

Piscataway Park is home to bald eagles, beavers, deer, foxes, ospreys, and many other species. To complement the surroundings, the park has, in addition to a public fishing pier and two boardwalks over fresh water tidal wetlands, a variety of nature trails, meadows, and woodland areas. The Park is also home to National Colonial Farm.

Seneca Creek State Park

11950 Clopper Road
Gaithersburg MD 20878
www.dnr.state.md.us/publiclands/central/seneca.asp
301.924.2127

The park, comprised of 6,300 acres, extends along 14 scenic miles of Seneca Creek, as it winds its way to the Potomac River. The Clopper Day-Use Area contains many scenic areas, including the 90-acre Clopper Lake, surrounded by forests and fields. Picnicking, boat rentals, trails, and a tire playground are just some of its recreational opportunities. A restored 19th century cabin and a self-guided path interpret the history of the area. Nearby, the Schaeffer Farm Trail Area offers 12 miles of marked trails for hiking and mountain biking. For the more adventuresome hiker, the 16.5-mile Seneca Creek Greenway Trail follows the entire course of the creek. About mid-May through June, the Schwartz peony gardens and field plants are in bloom.

Sligo Creek Park

Silver Spring MD 20902
www.montgomeryparks.org/PPSD/ParkTrails/trails_MAPS/sligo.shtm

This peaceful park, which runs through Silver Spring and Takoma Park, is a pleasant place to bike, walk, or have an old-fashioned family picnic. A hiking/exercise course, playground equipment, basketball courts, and a flat bike trail paralleling the creek for ten miles, make for a delightful family outing. Follow the trail to Wheaton Regional Park.

Sugarloaf Mountain

7901 Comus Road
Dickerson MD 20842
www.sugarloafmd.com/index.html
301.874.2024

A visit to Sugarloaf is a pleasant way for the family to enjoy nature. This privately owned mountain is known for its lovely foliage and vistas. The auto road goes almost to the top, and there are plenty of good walking and climbing trails to match your family's hiking levels. Young children can climb to the top from the auto road. More experienced climbers may want to ascend via "Devils Kitchen." There's a great view at the top and picnic spots scattered on the mountain.

Underground Railroad Experience Trail

16501 Norwood Road
Sandy Spring MD 20860
www.montgomeryparks.org/PPSD/Cultural_Resources_Stewardship/
heritage/urr_experience.shtm
301.650.4373

The two-mile long, wooded, scenic trail celebrates the history of the Sandy Spring Quaker community in helping to oppose slavery and commemorates the involvement of Montgomery County residents in the Underground Railroad, the system of the safe houses and brave "conductors" who helped slaves travel north to freedom.

IN VIRGINIA

Bull Run Marina

12619 Old Yates Ford Road
Clifton VA 20124
www.nvrpa.org/park/bull_run_marina
703.250.9124

This heavily wooded park on Lake Occoquan is an ideal spot for teaching children the art and lore of fishing (bait and tackle for fishing can be purchased in the park). Picnic tables and grills are scattered under the trees overlooking the water. The Marina has hiking trails and a playground, and offers outdoor education courses, as well as guided canoe trips.

Fountainhead Regional Park

10875 Hampton Road
Fairfax Station VA 22039
www.nvrpa.org/park/fountainhead
703.250.9124

Located at the widest point of Lake Occoquan, this scenic park is a conservation area that shelters a profusion of birds, geese, ducks, raccoons, deer, and other forest creatures. Picnic tables and grills overlook the water, and nature trails wind over hills and ravines to views of the lake and low marshlands. The park also offers miniature golf, and a five-mile mountain bike trail. It is an ideal spot to teach children to fish (licenses are sold at the park), and boats are available to rent. Access to the 17-mile Bull Run-Occoquan Trail is available.

Great Falls Park

9200 Old Dominion Drive
McLean VA 22102
www.nps.gov/grfa/index.htm
703.285.2965

Great Falls is an 800-acre park overlooking the magnificent Great Falls of the Potomac. Families come here to explore the remains of the 18th-century Patowmack Canal, built to bypass the falls, or to fish in the river. There are many hiking and equestrian trails, and a snack bar (open seasonally).

Huntley Meadows Park

3701 Lockheed Boulevard
Alexandria VA 22306
www.fairfaxcounty.gov/parks/huntley-meadows-park
703.768.2525

Nestled in Fairfax County's Hybla Valley, Huntley Meadows Park is a rich, natural and historical island of over 1,500 acres in the suburban sea of Northern Virginia. It harbors a nationally significant historic house, majestic forests, wildflower-speckled meadows and vast wetlands bursting with life.

Old Rag Mountain (Shenandoah National Park)

3655 Highway 211 East
Luray VA 22835
www.nps.gov/shen/planyourvisit/directions.htm
540.999.3500

A visit to the rocky top of Old Rag Mountain is a Green
Acres Middle School tradition. The mountain stands alone in
Virginia's Blue Ridge at 3,291 feet in a park filled with history
and surprises. Old Rag's Ridge Trail is a tough climb over and
through big boulders—but worth it for the spectacular views in
every direction. (You can see Skyline Drive to the west and the
Chesapeake Bay to the east.) This is a popular hiking spot; get
to the trailhead early in peak seasons. Two shelters on the circuit
have cooking fireplaces, though camping is not permitted above
2,500 feet.

Mason District Park

6621 Columbia Pike
Annandale VA 22003
www.fairfaxcounty.gov/parks/maps/masonmap.htm
703.941.1730

Mason District Park includes 121 acres in the heart of Fairfax
County. The park features tennis and basketball courts, ball
fields, and jogging trails. Visitors can enjoy a wildlife pond, take
a hike, or follow self-guided nature trails. There are picnic and
open play areas as well as a tot lot. An amphitheater offers a full
and varied schedule of day and evening programs in the summer.

Mount Vernon Trail

www.nps.gov/gwmp/planyourvisit/mtvernontrail.htm

This 18.5-mile trail is pleasurable for joggers, bikers, and
walkers. There are numerous interesting places to stop for a
picnic lunch or to take a rest. At Roosevelt Island, you can walk
the trails; LBJ Grove provides a clear view of the Washington
skyline; Gravelly Point is a favorite place to watch planes
take off and land; Daingerfield Island has water sports and a
restaurant; Dyke Marsh is a 240-acre wetland where you might
spot some rare species of birds.

Potomac Overlook Regional Park

2845 N Marcey Road
Arlington VA 22207
www.nvrpa.org/park/potomac_overlook
703.528.5406

On the Potomac Palisades in North Arlington, Potomac
Overlook offers 70 acres of peaceful woodland, trails,
educational gardens, a small picnic area and a Nature Center.
The Nature Center features the "Energerium," offering visitors
a fun and accessible way to learn energy basics and ways they
can help create sustainable energy solutions. The displays blend
lessons from ecology, Earth Science, physics, chemistry and
other topics in clear, understandable ways. The Nature Center
also houses live animals and natural history exhibits and is the
office for NVRPA's naturalist staff.

Prince William Forest Park

18100 Park Headquarters Road
Triangle VA 22172
www.nps.gov/prwi/index.htm
703.221.4706

Prince William Forest Park is an oasis, a respite of quiet and
calm. In 1936, Chopawamsic Recreation Area opened its gates
to house children's 'relief' camps during the Great Depression.
Renamed Prince William Forest Park in 1948, these fragrant
woods and trickling streams have welcomed generations of
campers, hikers, bikers, and nature lovers. Discover Northern
Virginia's best kept secret!

Red Rock Wilderness Overlook Regional Park

43098 Edwards Ferry Road
Leesburg VA 20176
www.nvrpa.org/park/red_rock_widerness_overlook
703.737.7800

Discover a beautiful, out-of-the-way place. Hike over hills and
through woods dotted with wildflowers to panoramic views of
the Potomac River and the distant mountains.

Riverbend Park

8700 Potomac Hills Street
Great Falls VA 22066
www.fairfaxcounty.gov/parks/riverbend
703.759.9018

Riverbend Park encompasses 409 acres of Potomac shoreline and has a Visitor's Center with a wooden deck overlooking the Potomac River. The park features picnic areas with grills, a snack bar, walking trails, and fishing. The Riverbend Nature Center (703.759.3211) has a naturalist staff, environmental exhibits, and many special programs.

Scotts Run Nature Preserve

7400 Georgetown Park
McLean VA 22102
www.fairfaxcounty.gov/parks/scottsrun
703.759.9018

Fairfax County naturalists refer to Scotts Run as the "Hot Spot for Wild Flowers," plus hiking, bird watching, and spectacular foliage. It is said that many of the huge trees are more than 100 years old. The scenery includes an abundance of dogwood and papaw as well as wildflowers in the spring. A three-mile trail follows a "stepping-stone stream" to a small waterfall and an awe-inspiring view of the Potomac. The trail gets more challenging as it approaches the river.

Theodore Roosevelt Island

George Washington Memorial Parkway
McLean VA 22101
www.nps.gov/this/index.htm
703.289.2500

From the parking lot, visitors cross over a footbridge to enter this 88-acre wildlife refuge, preserved in its natural state as a tribute to conservationist President Theodore Roosevelt. The deeply wooded island includes a clearing where a 23-foot bronze statue of Roosevelt rises from a plaza that incorporates small shallow pools. It is a pleasant place to rest or have a picnic lunch. The park boasts a vast variety of plants, beasts, birds, and bugs in the swamps and forests, and is a good place to fish as well as canoe (bring your own). Sturdy low-heeled shoes are a must for exploring the two and a half miles of foot trails that meander through the varied habitats. Insect repellent is recommended, especially in the summer.

Washington and Old Dominion Railroad Regional Park

21293 Smiths Switch Road
Ashburn VA 20147
www.nvrpa.org/park/w_od_railroad
703.729.0596

Called "the skinniest park in Virginia," this 45-mile strip of park follows the roadbed of the old W&OD Railroad. It is the most heavily used park in Northern Virginia. The 100-foot-wide paved path, which connects with numerous other trails and parks, serves bikers, hikers, joggers, and skate boarders from Arlington to Purcellville. The trail begins in Arlington, and there are several access points near Metro stations. Restrooms are located at several community centers along the way.

BATTLEFIELDS/HISTORIC SITES

Antietam National Battlefield

5831 Dunker Church Road
Sharpsburg MD 21782
www.nps.gov/ancm/index.htm
301.432.5124

The Visitors Center houses a small museum with period artifacts, and shows a 26-minute film every half hour that describes the battle of Antietam. A one-hour Antietam Documentary is shown daily at noon. For a more thorough understanding of the battle, rent the self-guided tour audiotape for $4 at the bookstore and drive around the battlefield. The eight and a half mile drive, with the tape, takes about two hours and includes 11 stops.

Ball's Bluff Regional Park

Ball's Bluff Road
Leesburg VA 20176
www.nvrpa.org/park/ball_s_bluff
703.737.7800

Interpretive signs with Civil War-era maps and photographs lead visitors along a trail into the days of the significant Battle of Ball's Bluff. The park encompasses much of the battlefield and surrounds the Ball's Bluff National Cemetery.

Fort Ward Park

4301 W Braddock Road
Alexandria VA 22304
www.alexandriava.gov/FortWard
703.746.4848

Fort Ward was the fifth largest of 68 Union forts built to defend Washington during the Civil War. Learn more about it at the park museum or enjoy the azalea and flower displays in the garden area of this 40-acre park. See also Fort Ward Museum on page 52.

Fort Washington Park

13551 Fort Washington Road
Fort Washington MD 20744
www.nps.gov/fowa/index.htm
301.763.4600

The present Fort Washington Park is a 341-acre natural area along the Potomac River. A large masonry Civil War Fort, it was completed in 1824 as the only permanent fortification built to defend the Nation's Capital. It is an outstanding example of early 19th-century coastal defense with its 45-foot high stone and brick walls sitting on a hillside above the Potomac River, and offers an excellent upriver view of Washington, DC. After viewing the movie in the Visitor Center and touring the Fort, you can enjoy a picnic lunch on the grounds. Features include trails, playgrounds, picnic areas, and other recreational and educational opportunities.

Fredericksburg and Spotsylvania National Military Park

120 Chatham Lane
Fredericksburg VA 22405
www.nps.gov/frsp/index.htm
540.373.6122

This national military park represents three years of war during the height of the Confederacy as well as the beginning of the final campaign of the Civil War where commanders Robert E. Lee and Ulysses S. Grant first met on the field of battle. Two visitors centers include museum exhibits, paintings, and audio-visual programs. There are four Civil War battlefields to tour, self-guided auto tours with numerous maps, and walking trails.

Manassas National Battlefield Park

12521 Lee Highway
Manassas VA 20109
www.nps.gov/mana/index.htm
703.361.1339

This park commemorates one of the first battles of the Civil War in 1861. The Visitors Center features a museum with a self-activating map program and a slide show every half hour. Ranger-guided tours are given during the summer, when the stone house is also open.

PICK YOUR OWN

Butler's Orchard

22200 Davis Mill Road
Germantown MD 20876
www.butlersorchard.com
301.972.3299

Families visiting the 300-acre Butler family farm will get an appealing and instructive view of fruits growing in the orchards and fields, and have an opportunity to pick their own produce. Kids of all ages will enjoy plucking the ripe fruit directly from the vine, tree, or bush. Bring your own baskets, which will be weighed before picking, or purchase them for a small fee. Fresh seasonal produce is also for sale at the stand.

Cox Farms

15621 Braddock Road
Centreville VA 20120
www.coxfarms.com
703.830.4121

Cox Farms is set on 116 acres overlooking a lake and the Blue Ridge Mountains. Offering seasonal farm market and greenhouse items, the farm is a child-friendly place with climbing structure and wagons for the children to use. It is open every day in October with extra activities on the weekends. The October theme is to experience harvest time at the farm. All activities center around outdoor physical activity in a rural environment such as pumpkin picking, hayrides, hay tunnels, mountain slide, and swings that drop into hay pits. Weekend festivals include food, face painting, and four stages with live entertainment. Cowboy Jake entertains live every day.

Homestead Farm

15604 Sugarland Road
Poolesville MD 20837
www.homestead-farm.net
301.977.3761

Homestead Farms is open in late May when the strawberries are ripe and ready to be picked. The summer season brings blackberries, peaches, and a variety of summer vegetables including vine ripened tomatoes and sweet corn picked fresh every day. At the farm market, you will find a large selection of jams and pickles as well as honey collected from beehives located on the farm. In mid-August, the red raspberry season begins, and later in the month, Gala apples are ready to be picked. These are the first of thirteen varieties of apples grown in the orchards. During the autumn harvest, Homestead's farm market is filled with apples, pumpkins, fall squash, Indian corn and fresh apple cider. No pets please.

Larriland Farm

2415 Woodbine Road
Woodbine MD 21797
www.pickyourown.com
301.854.6110

This 285-acre, pick-your-own produce farm is set in the rolling foothills of the Appalachian Mountains in Western Howard County. Sample fresh fruits and vegetables right in the field and take a hayride in October. With an 8-acre pond, woods, and a 125-year-old chestnut post and beam barn which houses a farm market, this is sure to be a delightful destination for the entire family. Please call ahead to verify specific hours and for listing of ripe fruits reading for picking. Containers are furnished. No pets please.

Potomac Vegetable Farms

9627 Leesburg Pike
Vienna VA 22182
www.potomacvegetablefarms.com
703.759.2119

This is a working, certified organic vegetable and berry farm with horses and chickens in a natural setting. The farm specializes in lettuce and greens, tomatoes, beans, squash, peppers, flowers and fresh eggs. Potomac Vegetable Farms also grows pumpkins and berries for pick-it-yourselfers. The proprietors encourage informal visits to their fields, animals, and ongoing operations. In addition to tours for young children, they also have tours for groups of older children who are interested in the connection between farming and the environment, health, and ecology issues. Bring your used egg cartons (in good condition) and plastic and paper bags to recycle.

GARDENS

Brookside Gardens

1800 Glenallen Avenue
Wheaton MD 20902
www.montgomeryparks.org/brookside
301.962.1400

This 50-acre public garden has outdoor plantings landscaped in formal and natural styles. In addition to the well-known azalea, rose, formal and fragrance gardens, there are aquatic and Japanese gardens with a Japanese teahouse. The lake is home to water snakes and fish. Geese and ducks can be found near the aquatic gardens, and butterflies are indeed attracted to the butterfly garden. Inside the two conservatories are colorful annuals and perennials and exotic plants. In the greenhouse, a stream with stepping stones is a delight for the little ones. Two annual exhibits are not to be missed: Wings of Fancy live butterfly exhibit runs from May to September, and the Garden of Lights runs from mid-November through early January.

Green Spring Gardens Park

4603 Green Spring Road
Alexandria VA 22312
www.fairfaxcounty.gov/parks/greenspring
703.642.5173

This park contains demonstration gardens for the home gardener, an extensively renovated 18th-century house, and the Horticulture Center with a greenhouse and a library. The grounds include formal rose, herb and vegetable gardens, a fruit orchard and an iris bed. Smaller children especially enjoy the woods and two ponds with ducks and geese. Horticulture classes are offered for children of all ages.

Kenilworth Park and Aquatic Gardens

1550 Anacostia Avenue NE
Washington DC 20019
www.nps.gov/keaq
202.426.6905
Metrorail Orange line (Deanwood)

Many varieties of flowering water plants thrive in the ponds of the Kenilworth Aquatic Gardens, a National Park Service site. Children love seeing the brightly colored flowers, watching frogs, turtles, birds, and fish in the ponds, and exploring the River Trail that borders the Anacostia River. Wildflowers begin blooming in the marsh in early spring, and the water lilies begin blooming in early summer.

McCrillis Gardens and Gallery

6910 Greentree Road
Bethesda MD 20817
www.montgomeryparks.org/brookside/mccrillis_gardens.shtm
301.962.1455

Five acres of shaded gardens, a small art gallery, benches, and a small pavilion make this a lovely place to visit. The gallery exhibits art in various styles and media by local artists. Bring bug spray in summertime!

Meadowlark Botanical Gardens

9750 Meadowlark Gardens Court
Vienna VA 22182
www.nvrpa.org/park/meadowlark_botanical_gardens
703.255.3631

This scenic public garden features 95 acres of natural and landscaped areas, a butterfly garden, herb garden, three wedding gazebos, three lakes and two miles of trails through woods, meadows and gardens. There are also three miles of paved trails, ideal for strollers and wheelchairs.

River Farm Garden Park

7931 E Boulevard Drive
Alexandria VA 22308
www.ahs.org/about-river-farm
703.768.7500

The elegant Main House at River Farm is set amidst 25 acres of lawns, gardens, meadows, and woods, and commands a sweeping view of the Potomac. Visitors can take self-guided tours of the Main House and the vast gardens. Of particular interest are the Children's Gardens with their unique designs: Butterfly, Dinosaur, Bat Cave, Alphabet, Boat, and Zig-Zag.

U.S. National Arboretum

3501 New York Avenue NE
Washington DC 20002
www.usna.usda.gov
202.245.2726

Enjoy the varied shrubs and trees, gardens, overlooks, and ponds as you explore this museum of living plants by road or footpath. It is most colorful in the Spring when thousands of azaleas are in bloom, but is enjoyable year-round, as there is always something blooming and plenty of "stretching space" for children to expend a little excess energy. Serious hikers will also find many intriguing trails throughout the Arboretum. A tram for touring the grounds is also available. By car, bus or bicycle there are nine miles of roadways that wind through and connect the numerous gardens and collections on the 446-acre campus.

REGIONAL PARKS AND PLAYGROUNDS

The Adventure Park at Sandy Spring Friends School

16701 Norwood Road
Sandy Spring, MD 20860
www.sandyspringadventurepark.org
240.389.4386

Located in the woods at the Sandy Spring Friends School, you will find this amazing "aerial forest park." Experience "adventure in the trees" on your own or with friends, family, and parties. With 13 Trails, 26 zip lines, 6 difficulty levels, and almost 200 challenge bridges, The Adventure Forest is the largest forest climbing park in the nation. Ages five to adult.

Algonkian Regional Park

47001 Fairway Drive
Sterling VA 20165
www.nvrpa.org/park/algonkian
703.450.4655

Located on the Potomac shore, this 800-acre park features a boat-launching ramp that provides public access to the wide Seneca Lake section of the Potomac River. Picnic tables are scattered under trees along the shoreline and covered shelters may be reserved for group picnics. There is also a snack bar on-site. Twelve riverfront cottages with three, four, or five bedrooms are available for rent as well as a Meeting Center/ Clubhouse. Visitors can enjoy fishing on the Potomac or playing miniature golf. In addition, there is an 18-hole, par-72 golf course. Also see, Downpour at Algonkian Regional Park, on page 146.

Allen Pond Park

3330 Northview Drive
Bowie MD 20716
www.cityofbowie.org/Facilities.aspx?Page=detail&RID=5
301.809.3011

Allen Pond Park offers a wide variety of activities guaranteed to make for a fun-filled day. Enjoy a picnic; play volleyball, softball, basketball, and horseshoes; play at Opportunity Park; go for a hike; and end the day with a sunset concert in the amphitheater (Sundays at 7 p.m., Memorial Day weekend-Labor Day weekend).

Audrey Moore/Wakefield Park and Recreation Center

8100 Braddock Road
Annandale VA 22003
www.fairfaxcounty.gov/parks/rec/moore
703.321.7801

Wakefield's 290 acres encompass both indoor and outdoor recreational facilities, including 11 lighted tennis courts, a lighted practice court, and shuffleboard. The indoor facility features a 50-meter pool, sauna and showers, weight room, gymnasium, dance and exercise rooms, game room, and courts for handball, squash, and racquetball. The 2,600 square foot mural in the pool area depicts a marvelous underwater world, including submerged towers of Atlantis. Visitors also enjoy the arts and crafts rooms as well as pottery and photography labs. Nearby is Wakefield Chapel, which was built in 1899 as an affiliate of the Methodist church. The chapel can be rented for appropriate community activities.

Bluemont Park

601 North Manchester Street
Arlington VA 22203
www.arlingtonva.us/Departments/ParksRecreation/scripts/parks/
bluemontpark.aspx
703.228.6525

Park facilities include basketball courts, baseball diamonds, athletic fields, lighted tennis courts (703.358.4747), and a soccer and softball area. There are also picnic areas with grills, playground equipment, and bicycle trails. The park connects to Four Mile Run bike trail. Bluemont's two best features are the nine-hole disc golf course and its stream, which is stocked for trout fishing at the end of March.

Brambleton Regional Park

42180 Ryan Road
Ashburn VA 20148
www.virginia.org/Listings/SportsVirginia/BrambletonRegionalPark
703.327.3403

Brambleton Regional Park is located along Belmont Ridge Road, adjacent to the National Recreation and Park Association. This facility includes two softball fields, four large baseball fields including field screens, bullpen, dugouts, concession stand, restrooms and water fountains. The park is open year round and features an 18-hole golf course.

Bull Run Regional Park

7700 Bull Run Drive
Centreville VA 20121
www.nvrpa.org/park/bull_run
703.631.0550

This park, deep in Civil War battlefield country, has 1,000 untouched acres of woods, fields, and streams. It is a sanctuary for small animals and a wide variety of birds. A half-acre outdoor fantasy pool complex is one of its chief attractions. The park offers a colorful new playground, miniature and disc golf, open play fields, tent and tent-trailer camping sites, picnic areas with grills, and some 18 miles of bridle paths. The "Blue Bell Walk" is a treat in spring when many wild flowers are in bloom. A sporting clays course, skeet, and trap shooting gallery, and indoor archery range help make this a park rich in activities to please virtually all interests.

Burke Lake Park

7315 Ox Road
Fairfax Station VA 22039
www.fairfaxcounty.gov/parks/burkelakepark
703.323.6600

Rent a rowboat, fish, or follow the trails around this 888-acre park. The marina rents boats and sells bait for fishing (spring-fall) in the 218-acre lake. This park has a five-mile walking trail, over 150 wooded campsites, and a camp store. For younger children, the park offers a miniature train, an old-fashioned carousel, a snack bar and ice cream parlor, and a playground. Picnic areas are plentiful in wooded spots. There is also an 18-hole, par-3 golf course (703.323.1641) and an 18-hole, disc golf course.

Cabin John Regional Park

7400 Tuckerman Lane
Bethesda MD 20817
www.montgomeryparks.org/facilities/regional_parks/cabinjohn
301.299.0024

Cabin John Regional Park is one of Montgomery County's biggest and best combinations of nature, sports and recreation. The park encompasses athletic fields, including the beautiful Shirley Povich Field; a full-service ice-skating rink; indoor and outdoor tennis courts; and many picnic areas, trails, and campsites. Kids of all ages can enjoy summer ball games and the miniature train that runs through the park. Many of the facilities are wheelchair accessible. From nature programs and hiking to playgrounds, sports and baseball—Cabin John has something for everyone.

Cameron Run Regional Park and Great Waves Water Park

4001 Eisenhower Avenue
Alexandria VA 22304
www.nvrpa.org/park/cameron_run
703.970.0767

This water-oriented park is tremendous fun for both children and adults. Cameron Run features a wave pool and a 3-flume, 40-foot high water slide. The wave pool is most appropriate for strong swimmers. Children under 13 must be accompanied by a person age 16 or older. Younger children will enjoy the creative play pool featuring giant water creatures, rain jets, and a shallow body flume. There is also a very shallow wading pool for the youngest children. Cameron Run has a sand volleyball court, batting cage, miniature golf course, picnic shelter for rent (703.352.5900), and a fishing pond.

Candy Cane City

7901 Meadowbrook Lane
Chevy Chase MD 20815
www.montgomeryparks.org/parks_facilities_directory/
meadowbrooklp.shtm
301.765.8700

With a variety of equipment to crawl through, slide down, climb on, and swing from, the Candy Cane City playground at Meadowbrook Park is a crowd pleaser for the very young. The name refers to the long ago time when the playground equipment was painted with red and white stripes. The elasticrete underneath helps cushion the feet and protect against injury. The adjacent recreation center, like other Montgomery County park centers, has ball fields, tennis courts, a well-equipped building, covered picnic area, a year-round activity program, and shaded play areas and water fountain.

Chinquapin Park Recreation Center & Aquatics Facility

3210 King Street
Alexandria VA 22302
alexandriava.gov/recreation/info/default.aspx?id=12352
703.746.5553

Chinquapin Park is a 44-acre park in the heart of Alexandria. It has a nature area and fitness trail, picnic tables, basketball and volleyball courts, lighted tennis courts, play module (handicapped accessible), and large open fields. The center offers a 25-meter indoor swimming pool with separate diving well, three racquetball courts, a fitness room, saunas, lighted outdoor tennis courts, a snack bar, and activity rooms.

Clemyjontri Park

6317 Georgetown Pike
McLean VA 22101
www.fairfaxcounty.gov/parks/clemyjontri
703.388.2807

Clemyjontri Park is a two-acre playground with carousel designed with the goal of creating accessible side-by-side play for all children of all abilities. The design incorporates four outdoor "rooms" surrounding a centerpiece carousel. The Rainbow Room archways and swings, the Schoolhouse and Maze, the Movin' Groovin' Transportation area, and the Fitness and Fun rooms are designed to include apparatus such as swings with high backs, some easy access, lower monkey bars, ramps that make all play areas wheelchair accessible, wide pathways between equipment and non-slip, porous surfaces to ensure greater access for all children. The carousel has chariots, a spinning teacup, prancing horses and is recessed to ground level for wheelchair access.

East Potomac Park

14th Street SW
Washington DC 20024
www.npca.org/parks/east-potomac-park.html
202.426.6841

For many locals, East Potomac Park is one of the city's best-kept secrets. This airy peninsula just south of the Jefferson Memorial drives a grassy wedge between the Potomac River and the Washington Channel. The park draws sports enthusiasts throughout the year. You'll find one 18-hole and two 9-hole public golf courses, miniature golfing, and a seasonal public pool. The scenic riverfront trail that winds around the park's perimeter is popular with walkers, runners, bikers, and skaters.

Fairland Recreational Park/Fairland Regional Park

3928 Greencastle Road
Burtonsville MD 20866
301.774.6255

This bi-county park includes more than 150 acres of parkland in Prince George's County and 322 acres in Montgomery County, and features attractions for a variety of recreational interests. Trails for walking and biking run through wooded hills and near streams. The aquatics center includes a heated, 50-meter, indoor pool with a moveable floor, a heated, indoor 25-yard leisure pool with a fountain, a heated whirlpool with waterfall, a family changing room, locker rooms with coin-operated lockers, and an outdoor deck area. The Sports and Aquatics Complex includes a gymnastics center, racquetball courts, a weight-training center, indoor and outdoor tennis courts, sand volleyball courts, and a 50-meter indoor swimming pool. The Gardens Ice House is located on-site, see page 137, as are the Fairland Batting Cages.

Hadley's Park

12600 Falls Road
Potomac MD 20854
www.montgomeryparks.org/parks_facilities_directory/fallsroadlp.shtm
301.765.8700

Hadley's Park is a one-acre fully accessible playground designed so children of all abilities can have fun and challenge themselves on its creative play course, featuring a soft-play surface ideal for roller-skates, bikes, and wheelchairs.

Hemlock Overlook Regional Park

13220 Yates Ford Road
Clifton VA 20124
www.nvrpa.org/park/hemlock_overlook
800.877.0954

Hemlock Overlook is an outdoor center offering a variety of outdoor and team development programs for students, teachers, businesses, teams, and churches. Activities are open to the public and special groups by reservation. Trails may be used without reservations.

Jefferson District Park and Golf Course

7900 Lee Highway
Falls Church VA 22042
www.fairfaxcounty.gov/parks/golf/jeffersongc
703.573.0444

This 60-acre park features a 9-hole executive golf course (par 35) and an 18-hole miniature golf course.

Lake Accotink Park

7500 Accotink Park Road
Springfield VA 22150
www.fairfaxcounty.gov/parks/lake-accotink
703.569.0285

The 77-acre lake is popular with fishing and boating enthusiasts. Rent a canoe, pedal boat, or rowboat, or take a ride around the lake on a tour boat. Boat launching and trout fishing are allowed from March–May and October–December. On land, children and adults enjoy miniature golf, nature walks, and biking trails. The park also features a carousel, playground, miniature golf, lovely picnic areas with tables, grills, and shelters (by reservation), a baseball field, and a basketball court.

Lake Fairfax Park

1400 Lake Fairfax Drive
Reston VA 20190
www.fairfaxcounty.gov/parks/lakefairfax
703.471.5415

This 476-acre park offers a 15-acre lake for boating (boat rentals and excursion pontoon boat rides available) and fishing, as well as a new water park, The Water Mine Swimmin' Hole (see page 150). Plan to spend an entire day at Lake Fairfax Park, starting with a few hours at the innovative pool with its numerous water slides and rambling river, followed by a ride on the miniature train and carousel. Rent a pedal boat and enjoy some quiet time on the lake, go for a hike on a nature trail, and enjoy a family picnic near playgrounds.

Lee District Park and Robert E. Lee Recreation Center

6601 Telegraph Road
Franconia VA 22310
www.fairfaxcounty.gov/parks/rec/leerec.htm
703.922.9841

The recreation center boasts a 50-meter indoor swimming pool with a water slide, fitness center, gymnasium, four racquetball/handball courts, saunas, and meeting rooms. In addition to the train and carousel, the park features playing fields, tennis courts, a tot lot, softplay indoor playground, a sand volleyball court, an amphitheater, and hiking trails.

Montrose Park

R Street NW
Washington DC 20007
www.montrosepark.org
202.426.6827

Open space provides room for games at this popular Rock
Creek Park location, featuring outdoor tennis courts (no
reservations needed), a boxwood maze, a playground,
and picnic tables. This is a nice place to visit after a trip to
Dumbarton Oaks (see page 23).

Norwood Local Park

4700 Norwood Drive
Bethesda MD 20815
www.montgomeryparks.org/parks_facilities_directory/norwoodlp.shtm
301.765.8700

This local park has been renovated to be a fully accessible
playground for kids of all abilities. Among the recreation
features this park offers are a playground, softball field, lighted
baseball field, and five tennis courts. The park also has a picnic
area and is home to the Norwood Recreation Building, which is
available for rent.

Occoquan Regional Park

9751 Ox Road
Lorton VA 22079
www.nvrpa.org/park/occoquan
703.690.2121

This spacious 400-acre park is scenically located on the Occoquan
River. The park offers 400 acres of recreational space, a touch
of the past with its historic brick kilns and reminders of the
women suffragists imprisoned here in the early 1900s. Features
include a batting cage, picnic tables, and walking trails.

Pohick Bay Regional Park and Golf Course

6501 Pohick Bay Drive
Lorton VA 22079
www.nvrpa.org/park/pohick_bay
703.339.6104

"Pohick," the Algonquin Indian word for "the water place," is an apt description of this 1000-acre waterside park. Visitors can swim, boat, canoe, kayak, and fish. Other activities include family camping (hot showers available), flying kites, miniature and disc golf, and picnicking. Golfers should find the 18-hole, par-72 course a challenge. The park also features a four-mile bridle path, hiking trails, and an observation deck that overlooks the Potomac River. Most of the area around the park is maintained as a wildlife refuge, and the recreation areas are planned to minimize the disturbance to the animals, especially the nesting area of the bald eagle.

South Germantown Recreational Park

18041 Central Park Circle
Boyds MD 20841
www.montgomeryparks.org/facilities/south_germantown
301.670.4660

South Germantown Recreational Park's Central Park features two championship miniature golf courses and a splash playground with a tumbling buckets waterfall, rain tree, water tunnel, and 36' water maze. The two 18-hole putting courses provide real challenges with water features, sand traps, rough turf, and natural obstacles that are part of the unique design. (The miniature golf season may extend beyond October, weather permitting.) National Youth Soccer League Championships games and some professional games are held here.

Tuckahoe Park and Playfield

2400 N Sycamore Street
Arlington VA 22213
www.arlingtonva.us/Departments/ParksRecreation/scripts/parks/
TuckahoePark.aspx
703.228.6525

This unique, creative playground features towers, tall slides, and a maze with special interest for 7-12 year olds. This wooded, well-loved park also has softball fields, a soccer area, lighted outdoor tennis courts, and picnic tables.

Turtle Park (aka Friendship Park)

45th and Van Ness Streets NW
Washington DC 20016
www.turtlepark.org
202.282.2198

Turtle Park is located in the American University Park neighborhood of northwest Washington, DC. Although its official name is Friendship Park, community members affectionately know it as Turtle Park because of the five large statues in the play area. The park is home to large enclosed play area with five play structures, swings, sand box and picnic tables, two basketball courts, two tennis courts, four baseball and softball fields, recreation center (with cooperative pre-school), and a spray park.

Upton Hill Regional Park

6060 Wilson Boulevard
Arlington VA 22205
www.nvrpa.org/park/upton_hill
703.534.3437

This park offers visitors a woodland oasis in the heart of the most populated area of Northern Virginia. Upton Hill has a large swimming pool complex with water park features and woodland nature trails. The popular miniature golf course in a garden setting features one of the longest miniature golf holes in the world. Other attractions include a gazebo, picnic areas, batting cage, Bocce ball court, horseshoe pit, and a playground.

Watkins Regional Park

301 Watkins Park Drive
Upper Marlboro MD 20774
www.pgparks.com/Things_To_Do/Nature/Watkins_Regional_Park.htm
301.218.6700

This 437-acre park offers a wide variety of activities from hiking and biking trails to a carousel and miniature golf to camping and athletic facilities—something to please every family member! The extensive playground has brightly colored equipment gentle enough for toddlers and challenging enough for 5-7 year olds. Additionally, Watkins Regional Park is home to Watkins Nature Center and Old Maryland Farm.

Wheaton Regional Park

2000 Shorefield Road
Silver Spring MD 20902
www.montgomeryparks.org/facilities/regional_parks/wheaton
301.680.3803

This 536-acre park is a great favorite with area residents. The park abounds with child-pleasing features, including a two-mile miniature train ride, a carousel, a four-mile paved bicycle trail (also excellent for strollers, wheelchairs, and skaters), two-mile hiking trails, fishing, ice skating, ball fields, horseback riding stables, and picnic areas.

NATURE CENTERS, PLANETARIUMS, AND SANCTUARIES

Arlington Public Schools Planetarium

David M. Brown Planetarium
1426 N Quincy Street
Arlington VA 22207
www.apsva.us/planetarium
703.228.6017

Used primarily for school programs during the day, this modern planetarium also offers a variety of public programs throughout the year including the monthly "Stars Tonight." In addition on select evenings the Friends of Arlington's Planetarium has programming for the public. See website for program details.

Brookside Nature Center

1400 Glenallen Avenue
Silver Spring MD 20902
www.montgomeryparks.org/nature_centers/brookside
301.946.9071

The nature center is part of the 536-acre Wheaton Regional Park. The nature center building houses live animal exhibits, the Children's Discovery Room, an observational bee hive, and wildlife exhibits. The center grounds include nature trails, a wooded nature play area, native plant gardens, an 1870s pioneer cabin, and accessible interpretive boardwalks.
The center is closed on Mondays; please check the website for additional information.

Clearwater Nature Center

11000 Thrift Road
Clinton MD 20735
www.pgparks.com/Things_To_Do/Nature/Clearwater_Nature_Center.htm
301.297.4575

Located in the Cosca Regional Park, this Nature Center offers a range of interpretive programs hosted by park naturalists. Visit the nature center with a small indoor pond to observe the live mammals, reptiles, amphibians, and birds of prey. Admission is free; check website for fees that apply to special programs. Groups of 10 or more may reserve a guided tour or other programs. (See Cosca Regional Park, page 63.)

Croydon Creek Nature Center

852 Avery Road
Rockville MD 20851
www.rockvillemd.gov/croydoncreek
240.314.8770

The Croydon Creek Nature Center is part of a 120-acre forest preserve just a short distance from downtown Rockville. Hiking trails allow you to explore the field, forest and stream surrounding this nature center. An Exhibit Room and Discovery Room provide interactive fun and educational environmental exhibits for all ages. The Discovery Room introduces children to the animals that live around Rockville and provides hands on activities. The Exhibit Room provides the opportunity to bird watch and to meet the Eastern Screech Owl. See website for details on special programs.

Gulf Branch Nature Center

3608 N Military Road
Arlington VA 22207
www.arlingtonva.us/departments/parksrecreation/scripts/nature/
parksrecreationscriptsnaturegulfbranch.aspx
703.228.3403

Located in a 38-acre wooded stream valley, this nature center features interpretive displays on Arlington and Virginia plants, animals, and natural history. The center includes a classroom, a children's Discovery Room, a pollinator garden, live animal exhibit room, a pond, a restored log cabin, an observation beehive, and a moderately strenuous 3/4-mile trail to the

Potomac River. Educational programs are offered year round to organized groups and the general public. Picnicking is allowed in the adjoining Old Glebe Park.

Hidden Oaks Nature Center

7701 Royce Street
Annandale VA 22003
www.fairfaxcounty.gov/parks/hidden-oaks
703.941.1065

The Nature Center is located in the 52-acre Annandale District Park and is ideal for children age 2 and older. Exhibits include small live animals such as turtles and snakes, a climbing tree (puppet/loft stage), a resource library and an urban woodlands interactive exhibit. Many of the exhibits provide "hands-on" options. The surroundings, including an oak forest, woodland stream, and traces of a Civil War railroad, as well as timbering and farming lands, make for an interesting visit.

Hidden Pond Nature Center

8511 Greeley Boulevard
Springfield VA 22152
www.fairfaxcounty.gov/parks/hidden-pond
703.451.9588

Acres of undisturbed woodland, quiet trails, splashing streams, and a tranquil pond are just a few reasons to visit Hidden Pond Park and Nature Center. Situated along the Pohick Stream Valley, the park offers solitude and opportunities for exploration and discovery. The Nature Center prepares the visitor for investigating and experiencing the ecology of ponds, streams, and wetlands. Exhibits include a live display of many of the inhabitants of the pond, a touch-table, a parent and child corner, and displays of "feature creatures" and current events in the natural world. The building also offers a lab/all-purpose meeting room for visiting school groups or special programs, and a small retail sales area with items for the nature lover. Outside, there are self-guided trails, which lead to the stream valley and surrounding woodlands. If treasure hunting is more your thing, the naturalists will gladly loan you nets, so you can go on your own to search in and around Hidden Pond. (Treasures must be returned to the pond before leaving.) Special events are offered year round.

Howard B. Owens Science Center and Planetarium

9601 Greenbelt Road
Lanham MD 20706
www.pgcps.org/~hbowens
301.918.8750

This modern science center emphasizes participatory exhibits and interactive programs. The Summer Science Enrichment Program is open to preschool through high school students on a first-come, first served basis. The center primarily serves students of the Prince George's County Public Schools.

Locust Grove Nature Center

7777 Democracy Boulevard
Bethesda MD 20817
www.montgomeryparks.org/nature_centers/locust
301.299.1990

This Nature Center has a small collection of nature books, games, puzzles, a tree exhibit, and some native snakes and frogs on display. There are several wooded trails for moderate hikes. A 1/4-mile trail leads to a naturalist garden and wildlife meadow. Another one-quarter-mile trail leaves the nature center and follows numerous steps downhill to a meadow that borders the Cabin John Creek.

Long Branch Nature Center

625 S Carlin Springs Road
Arlington VA 22204
www.arlingtonva.us/departments/parksrecreation/scripts/nature/
parksrecreationscriptsnaturelongbranch.aspx
703.228.6535

This Nature Center is situated in a hardwood forest with hiking and biking trails, swamp, meadow, and streams. The Washington and Old Dominion Bike Path (see page 72) passes through the area. The Nature Center offers many things for children and adults to explore, including displays of live reptiles and amphibians, an indoor turtle/fish pond, seasonal displays, and a discovery corner for young naturalists. Although most programs are free, reservations are required and can be made by calling the Nature Center.

Meadowside Nature Center

5100 Meadowside Lane
Rockville MD 20853
www.montgomeryparks.org/nature_centers/meadow
301.924.4141

This Nature Center is surrounded by 350 acres, including seven and a half miles of nature trails, a lake, marsh, pond, herb garden, raptor cage (with live owl, hawk, and turkey vulture), two butterfly gardens, and a mid-1800s farmstead. Inside the Center is a Curiosity Corner Room with a microscope table and many other interactive activities. There are live animal exhibits and a wildlife observation window as well. Legacy of the Land is a diorama of Maryland habitats. Kids love crawling into and sliding out of the cave and enjoy looking at an underground cross-section of the earth, which shows tree roots and a view into the bottom of a pond. Summer Conservation Clubs, adult volunteer program, and Junior Naturalist program are available.

National Wildlife Visitor Center, Patuxent Research Refuge

10901 Scarlet Tanager Loop
Laurel MD 20708
www.fws.gov/northeast/patuxent/vcdefault.html
301.497.5580

The $18 million National Wildlife Visitor Center is one of the largest science and environmental education centers in the Department of the Interior. Interactive exhibits focus on global environmental issues, migratory bird studies, habitats, endangered species, creature life cycles, and the research tools and techniques used by scientists. The Visitor Center offers wildlife management demonstration areas and outdoor education sites for school classes. Additionally, there are hiking trails, interpretive programs, tram tours, wildlife observations, and films. Take an interpretative tour around the refuge's Lake Reddington where you can see wildlife and evidence of wildlife activity. Learn about the habitats the refuge manages for the success of migratory birds, mammals, reptiles, amphibians, and more!

Peace Park/Kunzang Palyul Chöling

18400 River Road
Poolesville MD 20873
www.tara.org/visit-us/peace-park
301.710.6295

Kunzang Palyul Chöling is one of the largest communities of monks ordained in the Tibetan Buddhist tradition in North America. The beautiful temple complex is situated on 72 acres in rural Montgomery County, Maryland. It provides monastic living quarters for monks and nuns, a large wildlife refuge, peaceful walking trails, and 28 consecrated stupas. The 65-acre Peace Park is comprised of six gardens in which the traditional peaceful meditation is a clockwise 30-minute walk. The Prayer Room, with its twenty-four-hour-a-day prayer vigil, is also open to the public for meditation and prayer.

Rock Creek Nature Center and Planetarium

5200 Glover Road NW
Washington DC 20015
202.895.6070

One of the best in the area, this Nature Center offers many exhibits of the flora and fauna of its surrounding woodland. Children find the live reptiles and beehive especially interesting. There are also two self-guided nature trails.

The Nature Discovery Room contains hands-on activities, puppets, and books to help children learn about their environment. An exciting part of your visit to the Nature Center is the planetarium show. The room darkens, stars appear, and the audience is transported outdoors on a clear night. The show for the younger children concentrates on the identification of major constellations and the movement of the heavenly bodies through the night sky. The later show, for older children, is divided into a study of the sky as it will appear that night and an in-depth astronomy presentation. Evening stargazing sessions, run in conjunction with the National Capital Astronomers, are held approximately once a month, May through October. Also see Rock Creek Park on page 60.

Rust Sanctuary (Audubon Naturalist Society)

802 Children's Center Road
Leesburg VA 20175
www.audubonnaturalist.org/index.php/about-ans/sanctuaries/
rust-leesburg-va
703.669.0000

Located in Loudoun County, the Rust Sanctuary property includes a manor house, formally called Yoecomico, and 62 acres of land. Rust Sanctuary is committed to protecting the integrity of the natural area while providing opportunities and resources that encourage the discovery and appreciation of the natural world. The sanctuary protects six different kinds of habitats including: wildlife habitat gardens, meadows, hedge rows, mixed hardwood forest, pine plantation, and a pond. The manor house is equipped with offices, classrooms, meeting rooms, and a small nature center.

U.S. Naval Observatory

3450 Massachusetts Avenue NW
Washington DC 20392
www.usno.navy.mil/USNO
202.762.1467

The work of the U.S. Naval Observatory consists primarily of determining the precise time and the measurements of star positions. Tours include a short movie on the Observatory, a look at the highly accurate electronic clocks and other exhibits, and an explanation of the workings of the 12-inch Alvan Clark refractor telescope. On clear nights, the tours include a look through the telescope.

University of Maryland Observatory

3204 Metzerott Road
College Park MD 20740
www.astro.umd.edu/openhouse
301.405.6555

Looking through telescopes at stars, planets, nebulae, and galaxies makes for a fascinating visit at the University of Maryland Observatory. After a slide-show presentation on a topic of popular interest in astronomy, ranging from archaeo-astronomy to quasars, visitors get the chance to look at the sky through the observatory's four telescopes. A program

coordinator is available to answer questions and provide
assistance with the telescopes.

Webb Sanctuary (Audubon Naturalist Society)

12829 Chestnut Street
Clifton VA 20124
www.audubonnaturalist.org/index.php/about-ans/sanctuaries/
webb-clifton-va
301.652.9188

This 20-acre nature sanctuary has hiking and nature trails
through woods and meadows on rolling terrain outside the
quiet village of Clifton. Enjoy free programs or just to enjoy a
walk with nature! On the weekends you can take a self-guided
walk and look for resident and migrating birds, search for
salamanders, discover frogs and toads, or watch for butterflies
and wildflowers.

Woodend Nature Sanctuary (Audubon Naturalist Society)

8940 Jones Mill Road
Chevy Chase MD 20815
www.audubonnaturalist.org/index.php/about-ans/sanctuaries/
woodend-chevy-chase-md
301.652.9188

Woodend is a tranquil 40-acre wildlife sanctuary. The pond,
meadows, and woods are fun to explore; a self-guided nature
trail is available. Inside the main house is the Wilbur Fisk Banks
Bird Collection, consisting of 594 specimens, mostly from
eastern North America.

HISTORICAL FARMS

Carroll County Farm Museum

500 S Center Street
Westminster MD 21157
www.ccgovernment.carr.org/ccg/farmmus
410.386.3880

Visitors get a look back in history in this 1800s farmhouse
surrounded by 140 rolling acres of countryside. Guided tours
of the farmhouse; self-guided tours of the Living History Center
and exhibit buildings including a Spring House, Blacksmith
Shop, Tinsmith Shop, transportation exhibit, gardens, and

more. Farm animals stabled in the pasture area, a play area for
children, and nature trails are also available. Demonstrations
are scheduled throughout the season and may include quilting,
weaving, broom making, tinsmithing, and blacksmithing.
The General Store sells candy, souvenirs and handcrafted
items made by the resident artisans.

Claude Moore Colonial Farm at Turkey Run

6310 Georgetown Pike
McLean VA 22101
www.1771.org
703.442.7557

The Claude Moore Farm at Turkey Run is a living history
museum that portrays family life on a small, low-income farm
just prior to the Revolutionary War. The farm uses hands-on,
interactive programs to further the public's understanding of
agriculture and everyday life in 18th-century Virginia. This
unique opportunity to experience colonial history first hand
should not be missed!

Frying Pan Park, Kidwell Farm

2709 West Ox Road
Herndon VA 20171
www.fairfaxcounty.gov/parks/fryingpanpark
703.437.9101

This model farm of the 1930s offers urban children a rich
experience in rural living. Take a picnic lunch and spend some
time looking at this subsistence farm with its blacksmith shop,
historic schoolhouse, numerous farm animals, fields, farm
buildings, and horse arena.

Kiparoo Farms

3511 Bussard Road
Middletown MD 21769
www.kiparoofarmstudio.us
301.371.7454

A small family owned business located on a 158-acre working
sheep and dairy farm in rural Frederick County, Maryland.
Open every Saturday!

National Colonial Farm

3400 Bryan Point Road
Acookeek MD 20607
www.accokeekfoundation.org/tag/colonial-farm
301.283.2113

At this beautiful site on the Potomac, opposite Mount Vernon, the Accokeek Foundation, in cooperation with the National Park Service, has recreated a working farm. It features demonstration gardens and animals of a middle-class tobacco plantation in the 1770s. The farm includes a circa 1770 farm dwelling, an 18th century tobacco barn, and an out-kitchen. The National Colonial Farm is recognized as a leader in the field of historic plant preservation and grows historic varieties of field crops.

Oxon Hill Farm

6411 Oxon Hill Road
Oxon Hill MD 20745
www.nps.gov/oxhi
301.839.1176

Oxon Hill is a working farm with daily demonstrations of farm chores, animals, crops, and equipment typical of those on farms in the early 1900s. Children can pet the animals, and learn about animal care and farming methods. There are craft demonstrations, a natural spring, and a self-guided nature walk that explains how farms utilized the surrounding woods. An additional bonus—the spectacular view of the Potomac River, Washington, and Virginia.

Temple Hall Farm Regional Park

15855 Limestone School Road
Leesburg VA 20176
www.nvrpa.org/park/temple_hall_farm
703.779.9372

This self-sustaining 286-acre working farm raises farm animals (cows, goats, hogs, peacocks, chicken, ducks, and sheep) and produces Orchard grass and Alfalfa hay. Interpretive programs designed as outdoor classrooms are offered to educate children about the diverse aspects of farm life, animals, and crops. A farm interpreter leads tours and guides children as they participate in farm-related activities such as feeding the animals or working in the garden. All animals are in fenced pens; this is not a petting farm.

Walney Visitor Center/Ellanor C. Lawrence Park

5040 Walney Road
Chantilly VA 20151
www.fairfaxcounty.gov/parks/ecl/walney.htm
703.631.0013

A large preserve of open space, the park's 660 acres are home to many features including: the Walney Pond, various historic ruins, Walney Visitor Center, Cabell's Mill/Middlegate complex, picnic facilities, athletic fields and hiking trails. The Walney Visitor Center is a converted 1780 farmhouse with live animal exhibits, historical exhibits, greenhouse, and classrooms. The Walney house was a home to families who farmed the Walney farm during the 18th, 19th, and early 20th centuries. Outbuildings include a smokehouse, ruins of an icehouse and dairy complex, and demonstration gardens.

Sports and Recreation

SPECTATOR SPORTS

Baltimore Orioles

Oriole Park at Camden Yards
333 West Camden Street
Baltimore MD 21201
baltimore.orioles.mlb.com
410.685.9800 (Executive Offices)
888.848.BIRD (Tickets and Game Day Customer Service)

Glorious structure, good food, spectacular views...not to mention a celebration of America's pastime, Oriole Park at Camden Yards has inspired a generation of ballpark construction. Nestled into an historic neighborhood, the ballpark blends an old-fashioned sensibility with state-of-the-art facilities. A fun family outing, sure to inspire enthusiasm from the first-time or veteran fan! While you're there, visit the nearby Babe Ruth Museum.

Baltimore Ravens

M&T Bank Stadium
1101 Russell Street
Baltimore MD 21230
www.baltimoreravens.com
410.261.RAVE (7283)

The Ravens are Baltimore's pro football team, winner of the 2012 Super Bowl. They play eight home games a year. Tickets sell out fast, so please check the schedule and search for tickets before planning your outing!

Bowie Baysox

4101 Crain Highway
Bowie MD 20716
www.milb.com/index.jsp?sid=t418
301.805.6000 (Main Office)
301.464.4865 (Ticket Office)

This Class AA affiliate of the Baltimore Orioles plays approximately 70 games per year. Seeing the Baysox play is a chance to watch professional baseball inexpensively and comfortably. The fireworks on special occasions are said to be "better than the 4th of July." Mascot "Louie" is always on hand to accentuate the family atmosphere created at the ballpark. The stadium includes a kids' play area for additional fun, as well as group picnic areas. Check the website for schedule.

Cal Ripken Collegiate Baseball League

5804 Inman Park Circle #370
Rockville MD 20852
www.calripkenleague.org
301.793.1311

Enjoy a baseball game at one of the area's best fields for a family summer night. This amateur summer wooden-bat league presents promising college players, many from the DC/MD/VA area. The ballparks feature concessions, raffles, trivia contests, special activities for children, and best of all, that great hometown feeling

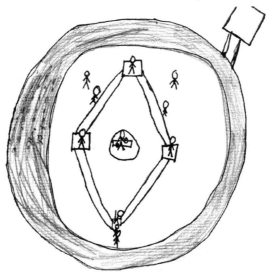

on game nights. Twelve local teams offer games across the region (Bethesda, DC, Alexandria, Gaithersburg, Rockville, Herndon, Baltimore, Silver-Spring/Takoma Park and more.) Check the website for links to specific teams, home field locations, and schedules.

DC United

RFK Stadium
2400 East Capitol Street SE
Washington DC 20003
www.dcunited.com
202.587.5000
Metrorail Blue and Orange lines (Stadium-Armory)

DC United has thrilled soccer fans in the nation's capital since the birth of Major League Soccer in 1996, earning domestic and international honors. A brand new stadium has been proposed for the team, so check website for up to date information on where the team will be playing.

Frederick Keys

Harry Grove Stadium
21 Stadium Drive
Frederick MD 21703
www.milb.com/index.jsp?sid=t493
301.662.0013 (Main Office)
301.815.9939 (Box Office)

The Frederick Keys baseball team is the Carolina League Class A Affiliate of the Baltimore Orioles. It is considered a high-quality farm team in the Carolina League. Some players become major league players! The Keys play 70 home games a season, so you have a good chance of finding a game scheduled when you are planning to visit the Frederick area.

Hagerstown Speedway

15112 Hagerstown Pike
Hagerstown MD 21740
www.hagerstownspeedway.com
301.582.0640

The Hagerstown Speedway is a true 1/2 mile track with straight-aways over 900 feet long & 70 feet wide. The track is 90 feet wide in the turns. The racing surface is made of the finest red clay in the nation. The smooth, wide surface makes

Hagerstown Speedway one of the fastest and safest dirt tracks in the U.S. on which to race.

Potomac Nationals

Pfitzner Stadium
7 County Complex Court
Woodbridge VA 22192
www.milb.com/index.jsp?sid=t436
703.590.2311

A Minor League baseball club, the Potomac Nationals are the Carolina League Class A Affiliate of the Washington Nationals.

Washington Capitals

Verizon Center
601 F Street NW
Washington DC 20004
www.capitals.nhl.com
202.628.3200 (Verizon Center)
202.397.SEAT (Tickets)
202.266.CAPS (Executive Offices)
*Metrorail Blue/Orange/Red lines (Metro Center); Green/Red/Yellow lines
(Gallery Place/Chinatown)*

Known to fans as "The Caps," this NHL hockey team thrills fans at the Verizon Center in the heart of Downtown DC.

Washington Nationals

Nationals Stadium
1500 South Capitol Street SE
Washington DC 20003
www.nationals.com
202.675.NATS (6287) (Offices)
888.632.NATS (6287) (Tickets)
Metrorail Green line (Navy Yard)

Major league baseball returned to Washington when the former
Montreal Expos relocated and took on the Nationals moniker
(after the nickname of the former Washington Senators). The
team's 2005 relocation to Washington was the first in Major
League Baseball since 1972. The 2008 season inaugurated
a state-of-the-art ballpark in Southeast Washington, along
the Anacostia River, with great views of the Capitol and the
Washington Monument.

Washington Redskins

FedEx Field
1600 FedEx Way
Landover, MD 20785
www.redskins.com
301. 276-6050 (Ticket Office)

The Redskins have been a DC institution since 1932. For nine
years in a row, the Redskins have broken the mark for single
season attendance! Their games at FedEx field are almost always
sold out so book any tickets well in advance! The Redskins are a
Green Acres favorite!

Washington Spirit

Maureen Handricks Field at Maryland SoccerPlex
18031 Central Park Circle
Boyds MD 20841
www.washingtonspirit.com
240.813.2693 (Field)
301.337.8579 (Tickets)

Come watch the Spirit, the DC region's newest professional
women's soccer team, play at the award-winning Maryland
SoccerPlex. Or watch the amateur Spirit Reserve team, formerly
known as DC United Women.

Washington Wizards

Verizon Center
601 F Street NW
Washington DC 20004
www.nba.com/wizards
202.661.5050 (Tickets)
202.661.5000 (Customer Service)
202.628.3200 (Verizon Center)
*Metrorail Blue/Orange/Red lines (Metro Center); Green/Red/Yellow lines
(Gallery Place/Chinatown)*

Once the Baltimore Bullets, then the Washington Bullets, this
NBA team settled into its current name and home in downtown
Washington in 1997. The team's roster has included three
players named to the list of the 50 Greatest in NBA History—
Earl Monroe, Wes Unseld and Elvin Hayes.

CANOEING, KAYAKING & SAILING

Belle Haven Marina

6401 George Washington Parkway
Alexandria VA 22307
www.saildc.com
703.768.0018

Belle Haven Marina is owned by the National Park Service; the
Mariner Sailing School there is owned and operated by sailors.
The rental fleet includes a 19-foot Flying Scots, 14-foot Sunfish,
kayaks, rowboats and canoes, as well as a 34-foot sloop with a
captain. The sailing school offers classes for adults and children
ages 8 and up. Classes are offered in April through October,
weather permitting.

Fletcher's Boathouse

4940 Canal Road NW
Washington DC 20007
www.fletcherscove.com
202.244.0461

Fletcher's Boathouse has been in operation since the mid-1800s.
Situated close to Georgetown, this landmark offers the perfect
embarkation point for renting bicycles, boats and canoes to
use on the Potomac and canal. You can also purchase fishing
licenses, bait, tackle, and cane poles to fish from the shoreline or

from the boats. Even though summer is the best time for many of the water activities, a walk in the woods in the wintertime from this point in the C&O National Park is memorable. Hours vary with the seasons and conditions; usually open dawn to dusk March through November.

Thompson Boat Center

2900 Virginia Avenue NW
Washington DC 20007
www.thompsonboatcenter.com
202.333.9543
Metrorail Blue Line (Foggy Bottom)

Enjoy a day on the Potomac River with Thompson's Boat Center. Bicycle rentals include all-terrains and cruisers. Boat rentals include kayaks, canoes and rowing shells. Instructional, recreational and community programs are available.

Washington Sailing Marina

1 Marina Drive at Daingerfield Island,
George Washington Memorial Parkway
Alexandria VA 22314
www.washingtonsailingmarina.com
703.548.9027

This George Washington Memorial Parkway/National Park Service concession is the place to rent a Flying Scot or Aqua Fin for a few hours for a sail around the lagoon, or to see Old Town Alexandria or Haines Point from the water. The Marina is home to three sailing clubs, and offers lessons and camps for all levels. Bike rentals are available year-round for a ride along the Mt. Vernon Bike trail, just adjacent to the marina.

EQUESTRIAN

Meadowbrook Stables

8200 Meadowbrook Lane
Chevy Chase MD 20815
www.meadowbrookstables.com
301.589.9026

Meadowbrook Stables is a hunter/jumper lesson and horsemanship facility, which offers a full lesson program for children and adults. Yearlong lesson programs are available, as are summer camps. The facility is also home to many "A" rated horse shows, and offers an Interscholastic Equestrian Association (IEA) team.

Potomac Horse Center

14211 Quince Orchard Road
North Potomac MD 20878
www.potomachorse.com
301.208.0200

This nationally-known riding school has three indoor arenas, two outdoor rings, and extensive trails, and offers lessons for children and adults of all levels. The center offers approximately 12 shows a year, as well as clinics, birthday parties, pony rides, trail rides, summer camps, and a therapeutic riding program. Horse boarding is also available.

Rock Creek Park Horse Center

5100 Glover Road
Washington DC 20015
www.rockcreekhorsecenter.com
202.363.0117

See beautiful Rock Creek Park by horseback! This horse center is DC's only full-service equestrian facility. Weekend and midweek guided trail rides are offered for riders 12 and older, and must be reserved in advance. Pony rides are also available for younger children. The center offers riding lessons for children and adults at all levels, from beginners through basic dressage, as well as camps for summer and spring break.

Woodland Horse Center

16301 New Hampshire Avenue
Silver Spring MD 20905
www.woodlandhorse.com
301.421.9156

Woodland Horse Center has a lighted outdoor ring, dressage ring and indoor ring, as well as riding fields and trail system. Woodland offers a complete program of equestrian activities, including grooming and working student programs, boarding, horse sales, and a fully equipped Tack Shop. While lessons are mainly English balance seat, Western lessons are available on a limited basis for adults only.

GOLFING AND MINI-GOLF

Brambleton Regional Park

42180 Ryan Road
Ashburn VA 20148
www.brambletongolfcourse.com
703.327.3403

Brambleton Regional Park is a championship 18-hole, par-72 golf course, with a full-service pro-shop. The course includes a variety of challenging holes, with scenic woods and water holes, large bunkers, and plush putting greens. Discounted Twilight rates available.

Monster Mini Golf, Gaithersburg

9116 Gaither Road
Gaithersburg MD 20877
www.monsterminigolf.com/fran-md-gaithersburg/index.html
301.330.6464

Come and experience 18 holes of fun-filled, indoor glow-in-the-dark, monster-themed mini golf. Best suited for the over 4 crowd.

Rocky Gorge 4 Seasons Golf Fairway

8445 Old Columbia Road
Laurel MD 20723
www.rockygorgegolf.com
301.725.0888

This golf and batting range is fun for the entire family. The driving range features sheltered tees (heated in winter and cooled by electric fans in summer), as well as a large putting green. Golf pros are also available for lessons. The 19-hole miniature golf range includes one of the world's longest miniature golf holes. The batting range boasts a 300-foot Home-Run Fence and sheltered cages for baseball or slow pitch softball.

Topgolf

6625 South Van Dorn Street
Alexandria VA 22315
www.topgolf.com/alexandria
703.924.2600

With nearly 80 covered and heated golfing bays, parents and children can experience a "near real" golf experience all year round in a fun game center equipped with the latest technology. Using real clubs and special golf balls embedded with computer chips to tee off from a driving bay onto a landscaped outfield with targets, players receive instant feedback from a computer screen in their bay.

Editors Note: *The above are just a small sampling of the golf and miniature golf options available in Maryland, Washington, DC and Virginia. For additional suggestions we recommend you check www.golflink.com which allows you to find courses by state or zip code.*

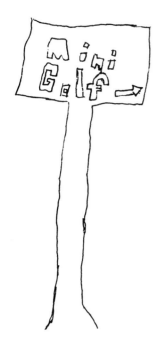

Arts and Entertainment

Whether you live around Washington or are visiting, be sure to take advantage of the city's many opportunities to introduce your children to the performing arts. You might want to explore options for finding lower-cost tickets. Here are a few ideas:

- TICKETplace offers half-price tickets that can be purchased on the day of the performance. Visit www.culturecapital.com for more information.

- Goldstar Events is a website offering half-price tickets for local theaters, concerts and sporting events. You will need to sign up to use the site, however. Visit www.goldstarevents.com/washington-dc/events for more information.

Adventure Theatre

Glen Echo Park
7300 MacArthur Boulevard
Glen Echo MD 20812
www.adventuretheatre-mtc.org
301.634.2270

Housed in the old Penny Arcade building of the historic amusement park, this children's theater—the Washington area's longest-running children's theatre—adds vitality to Glen Echo Park. Major productions year-round provide good professional entertainment. After the matinees, children can collect autographs from the performers and then run off for a ride on the carousel (Carousel open May through September, see Glen Echo Park on page 40). The Adventure Theatre Academy offers singing, dancing and acting classes for children, preschool through grade 12, at their Rockville location (Wintergreen Plaza).

American Film Institute; AFI Silver Theatre and Cultural Center

8633 Colesville Road
Silver Spring MD 20910
www.afi.com/silver
301.495.6700
Metrorail Red line (Silver Spring)

This three-screen complex offers a year-round program of the best in American and international cinema, featuring an eclectic mix of festivals, premieres, retrospectives, special events, tributes, on-stage guest appearances, and educational programs. The Educational Screening Program invites teachers to bring their classes (of all grade levels) free of charge to view films related to their curricula. The AFI was instrumental in the designation of Silver Spring as a Maryland Arts and Entertainment District.

Arena Stage

1101 6th Street SW
Washington DC 20024
www.arenastage.org
202.488.3300
Metrorail Green line (Waterfront)

Since reopening in 2010, the Arena Stage has become the second largest performance arts complex in the DC area, after the Kennedy Center. The complex, which houses three theaters, is a national center for the production, presentation, development, and study of American theater. While most productions are intended for adult audiences, programs for younger patrons include an after-school drama program for grades 8-11, and an interactive classroom or field trip program for preschool and kindergarten.

Arlington Cinema 'n' Drafthouse

2903 Columbia Pike
Arlington VA 22204
www.arlingtondrafthouse.com
703.486.2345
Metrorail Blue and Yellow lines (Pentagon City)

This historic 1930s Art Deco theater has been converted into a restaurant/theater with comfortable chairs and table-side service. The Drafthouse offers many family-friendly events, including movies, improvisational children's theater, magic shows, live music, and more. Family friendly events require that children under 21 be accompanied by a parent or guardian.

Blackrock Center for the Arts

12901 Town Commons Drive
Germantown MD 20874
www.blackrockcenter.org
301.528.2260

This center provides venues for performances in music, dance and theater along with film presentations, lectures, gallery exhibits, and arts education. Programming includes many family-friendly performances. Classes in the performing, literary and visual arts are offered for children, teens and adults.

Encore Stage and Studio

Thomas Jefferson Community Theatre
125 South Old Glebe Road
Arlington VA 22204
www.encorestageva.org
703.548.1154
Metrorail Orange line (Ballston)

This children's theater offers fully staged and beautifully costumed musicals and dramas for children by children. Some are original, some are traditional, but all are performed by talented young actors.

Open auditions are held for each production. A variety of classes and camps are also offered for grades K through 12. After school classes are located at a second Arlington location (3700 S. Four-Mile Run Drive).

The Comedy Spot/Comedy Sportz

Ballston Common Mall
4238 Wilson Boulevard
Arlington VA 22203
www.comedyindc.com
703.294.5233
Metrorail Orange line (Ballston/MU)

The Comedy Spot offers weekly live comedy shows, both family-friendly and adults-only. ComedySportz is a clean, family-friendly improv show. The kids' version, Comedy

Sportz4Kids, actually makes your kids the stars! You can book a party too.

Fairfax Symphony Orchestra

3905 Railroad Avenue (Administrative Offices)
Fairfax VA 22030
www.fairfaxsymphony.org
703.563.1990 (Administrative Offices)

Performance Location:
George Mason Center for the Arts
4373 Mason Pond Drive
Fairfax VA 22030
cfa.gmu.edu
888.945.2468 (Ticket Sales)

Each summer, the Fairfax Symphony performs free, family-friendly concerts at various locations throughout the area. Performances feature a mix of folk, contemporary, and classical music. The Symphony's educational programs include Overture to Orchestra (which introduces elementary grades to different instruments and sounds through in-school concerts) and SCORE (which offers master classes, individual sectional instruction, and side-by-side rehearsals to middle- and high-school bands and orchestras).

Folger Shakespeare Theatre

201 East Capitol Street SE
Washington DC 20003
www.folger.edu
202.544.4600 (Administrative Offices)
202.544.7077 (Box Office)
Metrorail Blue and Orange line (Capitol South); Red line (Union Station)

This 250-seat theater is constructed to suggest an open-air 17th-century theater, and is home to three Shakespeare and contemporary themed productions each year. Check the website for special family programming.

Imagination Stage

4908 Auburn Avenue
Bethesda MD 20814
www.imaginationstage.org
301.280.1660 (Box Office)
301.961.6060 (Information)
Metrorail Red line (Bethesda)

Imagination Stage is the largest multi-disciplinary theatre arts organization for young people in the region. The Imagination Stage season offers professional shows for families as well as year-round classes, performance opportunities, and school outreach programs for young people. Imagination Stage is committed to making the arts inclusive and totally accessible to all children regardless of physical, cognitive, or financial abilities. The facility includes a 364-seat main theater and a 142-seat black box theater, along with studios, birthday party room, a café, and a gift shop.

July Fourth Concert at the U.S. Capitol

202.554.4620
www.pbs.org/capitalfourth

"A Capitol Fourth" is a televised family-friendly Fourth of July concert on the West Lawn of the U.S. Capitol, featuring an all-star cast in a patriotic evening of musical performances. The concert is capped off with a rousing rendition of Tchaikovsky's "1812 Overture" complete with live cannon fire provided by The U.S. Army Presidential Salute Battery, and an unparalleled view of the fireworks over the Washington Monument. The 8:00 PM event is open to the public; no tickets are required. Gates typically open at 3:00 PM, but check the website for the exact time, as well as for a list of what is allowed or prohibited at the Capitol. Dance, sing, and wave your red, white, and blue and you might just end up on TV!

The John F. Kennedy Center for the Performing Arts

2700 F Street NW
Washington DC 20566
www.kennedy-center.org/index.cfm
202.467.4600; 800.444.1324
Metrorail Blue and Orange lines (Foggy Bottom/GWU)

The Kennedy Center is America's living memorial to President Kennedy and home to six theaters that host great artists and performances of music, dance, and theater from around the world. Offerings include National Symphony Orchestra concerts, plays and musicals, opera, ballet and modern dance, jazz and chamber music, performances for young people, films, and more. Check website for family-friendly programming including free daily performances on the Millennium Stage.

Marine Barracks Evening Parade

8th and I Streets SE
Washington DC 20390
www.barracks.marines.mil/Parades/EveningParade.aspx
202.433.4073 / 74
Metrorail Blue and Orange lines (Eastern Market)

A one hour and fifteen minute performance of music and precision marching, the Evening Parade features the U.S. Marine Band, the U.S. Marine Drum and Bugle Corps, the Marine Corps Color Guard, the Marine Corps Silent Drill Platoon, ceremonial marchers, and Lance Cpl. Chesty XIII, the official mascot of the Marine Barracks Washington. It is an impressive spectacle and a wonderful way to spend a summer evening. Parades held Friday evenings at 8:45, May-August (For guaranteed seating, make reservations and arrive between 7:00 and 7:45). No food or beverage other than water and baby food allowed.

Maryland Hall for the Creative Arts

801 Chase Street
Annapolis MD 21401
www.marylandhall.org
401.263.5544 (Main Office)
410.280.5640 (Box Office)

Visit this home to the arts in Anne Arundel County featuring live theatre, music and dance performances, hands-on art activities, gallery exhibitions and classes for children and adults. Many performances are designed for younger audiences.

Military Band Summer Concerts

U.S. Capitol Building (West front). Other performance locations include Yards Park, Capitol riverfront, Marine Barracks of Washington, Ft. Myer, and Navy memorial.

www.usarmyband.com/event-calendar.html
www.navyband.navy.mil/cota.shtml
www.marineband.marines.mil/Calendar.aspx
www.usafband.af.mil/Calendar/default.aspx

The Army, Navy, Marine Corps, and Air Force bands perform on alternating days throughout the summer. Concerts are free and no tickets are required. Check websites for schedule and locations.

Montgomery College Robert E. Parilla Performing Arts Center

51 Manakee Street
Rockville MD 20850
www.montgomerycollege.edu/pac
240.567.5301
Metrorail Red line (Rockville)

The Saturday Morning Children's Series held at this Montgomery College performing arts center features four to five musical theater events each year, based on books for young audiences. Designed for short attention spans, these performances are 50-60 minutes long.

Mosaic District Family Events

2910 District Avenue
Fairfax, VA 22031
www.mosaicdistrict.com
703.992.7765

Northern Virginia's new family destination with great restaurants, local boutiques, interactive fountains, and amazing community events. Stories from Strawberry Park, at the Angelika Theater, presents an interactive storytelling performance for kids 10 and under. Cartoons and Coffee and Films in the Park show films on the huge outdoor screen. Stroller Rides offers a fitness program, taught by certified instructors, that moms and dads can do with their babies (complete with songs and activities to engage the little ones).

Mount Vernon Community Children's Theatre

1900 Elkin Street, Suite 225 (Administrative Offices Only)
Alexandria VA 22308
www.mvcct.org
703.360.0686

Mount Vernon Community Children's Theater (MVCCT) has
presented theatrical productions featuring young actors from
the Washington metropolitan community since its incorporation
in 1980. Performed by children for children, MVCCT has
consistently won awards for its productions and programs.
Workshops, classes, summer camp, and full-scale productions
of musicals and dramas fulfill the theater's mission to provide
opportunities for children to participate in the creative process
of live theater. See website for performance locations.

National Gallery of the Arts Film Program

401 Constitution Avenue NW
Washington DC 20565
www.nga.gov/content/ngaweb/education/families/film.html
202.789.3030
*Metrorail Blue line (Smithsonian); Green and Yellow lines (Archives-Penn
Quarter-Navy Memorial); Red line (Judiciary Square)*

The Children's Film Program offers innovative programming
and fosters an understanding of film as an art form. The
program presents a broad range of foreign and domestic films,
including a variety of animation styles, live-action and classics.
All programs are shown in the East Building Auditorium, unless
otherwise noted. Programs are free and seating is offered on a
first-come, first-serve basis. No food or drink permitted.

The National Theatre

1321 Pennsylvania Avenue NW
Washington DC 20004
www.thenationaldc.com/tickets/childrens-programming
202.628.6161
Metrorail Blue/Orange/Red lines (Metro Center)

For almost 200 years, the historic National Theatre has
occupied a prominent spot on Pennsylvania Avenue and has
been considered the historic cultural center of the performing
arts in the nation's capital. General programming includes

Broadway shows, classic movies, and Community Vaudeville. Children's programming includes free Saturday morning performances. These dynamic one-hour shows invite audience participation and are irresistible to kids age four and older. Magicians, dancers, mimes, and puppets are among the top performers of local and national renown. Seating is limited, and tickets are distributed 30 minutes before each show.

National Zoo Concerts

3001 Connecticut Avenue NW
Washington DC 20008
www.nationalzoo.si.edu/events/default.cfm
202.633.4888
Metrorail Red line (Woodley Park/Zoo or Cleveland Park)

Come on over to the wild side and hear music among the animals…check the zoo's website for periodic musical performances and other programming.

Netherlands Carillon Concerts

George Washington Memorial Parkway VA
www.nps.gov/gwmp/planyourvisit/carillon_concerts.htm
703.289.2500
Metrorail Blue and Orange lines (Rosslyn Metro); Blue line (Arlington National Cemetery)

Come sit on the grass to hear the free carillon concerts of jazz, pop, and patriotic music. A gift from the people of the Netherlands, the 50-bell carillon, housed in its open steel structure, is an impressive auditory and visual experience. Visitors may go up into the tower to watch the carillonneur perform and to view the city of Washington. Live concerts are performed on Saturdays and holidays from May to September. Automated concerts daily at noon and 6 p.m. Parking is available at The U.S. Marine Corps War Memorial.

Now This! Kids!

www.nowthisimprov.com
202.364.8292

Now This! Kids! presents a delightfully innovative and totally improvisational show appropriate for children ages 5-12. Every skit is an original, based on suggestions from the audience with funny and amazing results. This traveling troupe will come to your event. Or, you can come to their weekly Saturday performance at Blair Mansion in Silver Spring, MD. Party packages and group rates are available.

Olney Theater Center

2001 Olney-Sandy Spring Road
Olney MD 20832
www.olneytheatre.org
301.924.4485 (Administrative Office)
301.924.3400 (Box Office)

The Olney Theatre Center is a professional theater with four performing venues, including seating for up to 500 on the west lawn for the theater's Summer Shakespeare Festival. The season includes staging of classic and contemporary plays, some for family audiences.

Potomac Overlook Regional Park's Summer Concert Series

2845 Marcey Road
Arlington, VA 22207
www.nvrpa.org/park/potomac_overlook/content/concerts

This concert series features a mix of folk, bluegrass, contemporary, and classical music. Performances are every other Saturday. Visit the web site for a summer schedule. Picnics are welcome, but no alcohol allowed. See page 70 for more information about Potomac Overlook Regional Park.

Prince George's Publick Playhouse for the Performing Arts

5445 Landover Road
Cheverly MD 20784
arts.pgparks.com/Our_Facilities/Publick_Playhouse.htm
301.277.1710

The Playhouse, originally the 1947 art deco Cheverly Theatre, was renovated and reopened in 1975 as a theater committed to cultural diversity in the arts. Known throughout the metropolitan area for the quality and affordability of its programs, this 462-seat theatre features nationally recognized touring companies in dance, music and theater, and is home to many community arts groups.

Puppet Company Playhouse

Glen Echo Park
7300 MacArthur Boulevard
Glen Echo MD 20812
www.thepuppetco.org
301.634.5380

The Puppet Company performs delightful productions with
clever interpretations of many children's classics. These critically
acclaimed and award-winning puppet shows incorporate hand
puppets, rod puppets, marionettes, masks, and costumed figures.
Shows are held at the Puppet Co. Playhouse at Glen Echo
Park. See a Main Stage production, or a Tiny Tots production,
especially designed for kids 0-4 years (shorter shows, lighted
room, open doors).

Round House Theatre

Bethesda Theatre location:
4545 East West Highway
Bethesda MD 20814
Metrorail Red line (Bethesda)

Silver Spring Theatre location:
8641 Colesville Road
Silver Spring MD 20910
Metrorail Red line (Silver Spring)

www.roundhousetheatre.org
240.644.1099 (Administrative Offices)
240.644.1100 (Box Office)

Round House offers a variety of stage productions each season,
exploring different forms of theater and performing arts.
Limited engagements, contemporary adaptations of the classics,
world premieres, and works-in-progress can all be found on
the stages at Bethesda and Silver Spring. Classes and camps are
available for all ages at a separate Education Center location in
Silver Spring.

Shakespeare Theatre Company

Sidney Harman Hall location:
610 F Street NW
Washington DC 20004
Metrorail Red line (Judiciary Square); Red/Green/Yellow lines (Gallery Place/Chinatown)

Landsburgh Theatre location:
450 7th Street NW
Washington DC 20004
Metrorail Green/Red/Yellow lines (Gallery Place/Chinatown); Green/Yellow lines (Archives-Navy Memorial-Penn Quarter)

www.shakespearetheatre.org
202.547.1122 (Box Office)

The Harman Center for the Arts opened in 2007 to combine the Lansburgh Theatre and Sidney Harman Hall, home of the Shakespeare Theatre Company. The Center provides a Washington venue for local, national and international performing arts companies.

Smithsonian Discovery Theater

1100 Jefferson Drive SW
Washington DC 20024
www.discoverytheater.org
202.633.8700
Metrorail Blue and Orange lines (Smithsonian)

Discovery Theater has been presenting DC-area children with live educational performances for more than 30 years. Shows, which run 40-50 minutes at various locations throughout the Smithsonian, present accurate and entertaining programs for experiencing heritage, science and culture. Touring shows are also available for booking at schools or libraries.

Strathmore

Mansion at Strathmore
10701 Rockville Pike
North Bethesda, MD 20852

Music Center at Strathmore
5301 Tuckerman Lane
North Bethesda, MD 20852

www.strathmore.org
301.581.5100 (Ticket Office)
301.581.5108 (Tea Reservations)
301.581.5200 (Administrative Offices)
Metrorail Red line (Grovesnor)

From large, world-class performances in the Music Center to more intimate performances in the Mansion, to gallery exhibits, lectures and the outdoor sculpture garden, all housed on the scenic 11-acre site, Strathmore provides a wide range of arts programming for all ages. Family favorites include summertime performances at the Backyard Theater Stage, the Outdoor concert series, and child-themed afternoon teas in the Mansion. Check out their educational programs too.

Synetic Theater

1800 South Bell Street
Arlington VA 22202
www.synetictheater.org
703.824.8060 (Administrative Offices)
866.811.4111 (Box Office)
Metrorail Blue and Yellow lines (Crystal City Metro)

This children's theater offers wonderful productions geared to children ages 4-12+. The company comprises professional actors trained in movement and Eastern European-style acting. Plays often include puppets as well as actors. In addition to performances at their intimate 75-seat theater in Arlington, the company has also brought plays to the National Theatre in Washington and to the Arts Barn Theatre in Gaithersburg. The Theater offers classes and summer camps in performing and visual arts.

Toby's Dinner Theatre

5900 Symphony Woods Road
Columbia MD 21044
www.tobysdinnertheatre.com
301.596.6161

Since 1979, Toby's Dinner Theatre of Columbia has brought "the best of Broadway" and original musicals to a modern theatre-in-the-round. One of only a few regional dinner theatre venues with a live orchestra, Toby's offers a number of family-friendly musicals each year.

Union Market

1309 5th Street NE
Washington, DC 20001
www.unionmarketdc.com

Union Market is a year-round, indoor, artisanal market with over 40 vendors providing the highest quality of local goods in the District. In addition to being a great place for families any day of the week, the market also has a number of kid-friendly events and programming. Try DC Drive-In and The Annual DC Scoop Ice Cream Festival in the summer months. The market also hosts Boogie Babes, live musical performances for kids and their grown-ups, every Wednesday at 10:30. (The cost is generally $5 per child and siblings under 6 months free)

The Washington Ballet

3515 Wisconsin Avenue NW
Washington DC 20016
www.washingtonballet.org
202.362.3606
Metrorail Red line (Tenleytown or Cleveland Park)

The Washington Ballet @ THEARC
1901 Mississippi Avenue SE
Washington DC 20020
www.thearcdc.org/partners-programs/washington-ballet
202.889.8150
Metrorail Green line (Southern Avenue)

While many of the Washington Ballet's performances at the Warner Theater, the Harman Center, and Kennedy Center are meant for adults the troupe offers intimate performances in its studios that appeal to boys and girls of all ages. Kids are wowed by the close proximity to the dancers, who may be no more than 10 feet away, and enjoy the behind-the-scenes atmosphere that allows them to watch muscular men and graceful women warm up at the barre. Ballets are performed to music that ranges from Bach to the Beatles to the Blues. The Washington School of Ballet offers a wide range of classes from pre-ballet for 6-year-olds to pre-professional for teens serious about a ballet career. The school also offers special classes for boys as well as for adults.

Wolf Trap

1551 Trap Road
Vienna VA 22182
www.wolftrap.org
703.255.1900 (General Information)
877.965.3872 (877.WOLFTRAP)
Shuttle available from Metrorail Orange line (West Falls Church-VT/UVA)

Wolf Trap is America's only national park for the performing arts and includes a number of venues. The Filene Center, surrounded by 100 acres of rolling hills, woods, and streams, combines under-the-roof and under-the-stars seating. Resident professional companies, as well as world-renowned artists, perform during the summer. During the fall and winter, performances are scheduled in the Barns at Wolf Trap. A wide variety of programs, from folk singing to jazz, are offered. Theatre in Woods, a summertime favorite, brings high-profile artists to perform for children in preschool and elementary school. Classes available for all ages.

FESTIVALS

Whether you are living in or visiting the Washington, DC area, you should know about the many festivals and fairs across the region, the majority of which tend to be kid-friendly. We will highlight a few of the bigger ones, but take the time to investigate all that this region has to offer.

Cherry Blossom Festival

www.nationalcherryblossomfestival.org

The National Cherry Blossom Festival is Washington, DC's and the nation's greatest springtime celebration that annually celebrates the gift of the cherry blossom trees and their symbol of enduring friendship between the citizens of Japan and the United States. Timed in conjunction with the peak blooming period of the trees, the city-wide event attracts visitors and area residents to hundreds of events in partnership with more than 30 local organizations.

National Book Festival

www.loc.gov/bookfest

Held each Fall, this festival celebrates everything and anything to do with books! The festival features authors, poets and illustrators in several pavilions. Festival-goers can meet and hear firsthand from their favorite poets and authors, get books signed, hear special entertainment, have photos taken with storybook characters and participate in a variety of activities. One pavilion is entirely devoted to children's literature.

Smithsonian Folklife Festival

www.festival.si.edu

At the annual Smithsonian Folklife Festival, held during summer, you will find many exemplary practitioners of diverse, authentic, living traditions—both old and new. The goal of the Festival is to strengthen and preserve these traditions by presenting them on the National Mall. Tradition-bearers and the public can connect with and learn from one another and, in a respectful way, begin to understand cultural differences and similarities.

International Children's Festival

www.artforculturaldiplomacy.com/component/k2/item/428-international-childrens-festival

Each May, the Meridian International Center hosts an International Children's Festival in Washington, DC promoting cultural exchange and introducing families to world geography, dress, and traditions. The festival is a part of Passport DC, an annual event featuring open houses at DC's embassies. More than 25 embassies host educational booths that highlight their countries' rich cultural heritage through hands-on activities, demonstrations, tastings, and a wide range of musical and dance performances, as well as an international children's parade.

USA Science and Engineering Festival

www.usasciencefestival.org

This festival is part of a national grassroots effort to advance STEM education and inspire the next generation of scientists and engineers. The exhibitors, performers, speakers, partners, sponsors and advisors are a who's who of science and engineering in the United States: from major academic centers and leading research institutes and government agencies to cutting-edge high tech companies, museums and community organizations.

This is, of course, just a small sampling of the fun to be had with your family! From summer street fairs to free outdoor summer movies to jazz festivals, there is always something exciting going on in Washington, DC, as well as in Maryland and Virginia. For some additional resources we recommend the following websites:

www.culturecapital.com

www.kidfriendlydc.com

www.washingtonparent.com

Books and Toys

A Likely Story Children's Bookstore

7566 Main Street
Sykesille MD 21784
www.sykesvillebooks.com
410.795.1718

This independent bookstore, located in historic downtown Sykesville, offers an eclectic mix of books, both new and used, in all genres. Shop for cards, journals, toys and games too.

Audubon Naturalist Sanctuary Shop

8940 Jones Mill Road
Chevy Chase MD 20815
www.audubonnaturalist.org/index.php/support-ans/shop
301.652.3606

Located at Woodend, the home of the Audubon Naturalist Society, this shop stocks an extensive selection of books on animals and plants, nature books for children, unusual puppets and puzzles, nature games, and birding supplies. You might want to schedule your visit to coincide with the beginners' bird walk. A visit at any time can include a walk on the trails of Woodend's 40 acres, which border Rock Creek Park.

Barnes and Noble

www.barnesandnoble.com

Barnes and Noble offers a broad selection of books, with over 175,000 titles in stock, and an extensive children's department. Children's events, such as author visits, story times, and children's activities, are scheduled regularly, as well as adult functions, such as book discussion groups and author appearances. This is a peaceful place to browse, have a cup of coffee, and enjoy the ambiance of fine literature all around. Locations throughout Washington, DC, Maryland and Virginia.

Barston's Child's Play

Northwest DC location:
5536 Connecticut Avenue NW
Washington DC 20015
202.244.3602

McLean location:
1382 Langley Shopping Center
McLean VA 22101
703.448.3444

Rockville location:
Congressional Plaza
1661 Rockville Pike
Rockville MD 20852
301.230.9040

Baltimore location:
Village of Crosskeys
86 Village Square
Baltimore MD 21210
410.435.0804

Arlington location:
4510 Lee Highway
Arlington VA 22207
703.522.1022

This popular toy store, well known for its extremely knowledgeable and helpful staff and fine selection of toys, has added new locations in recent years and has expanded its children's book department. The staff provides excellent guidance for choosing just the right gift!

Fairy Godmother

319 7th Street SE
Washington DC 20003
202.547.5474
Metrorail Blue and Orange lines (Eastern Market)

This children's bookstore on Capitol Hill carries a wide range of fiction and non-fiction for infants through teens, as well as foreign language children's books and CDs. It also has a large selection of creative toys and art materials, music CDs and cassettes, book-related videos and stuffed animals. The store will special order any items not in stock.

Kinder Haus Toys

1220 North Fillmore Street
Arlington VA 22201
www.kinderhaus.com
703.527.5929
Metrorail Orange line (Clarendon)

This independently owned store features a well-considered selection of fine children's toys, including a great selection of wood toys and Folkmanis puppets, as well as books and crafts, and children's clothing and shoes. The Imagination Station department carries a large selection of children's books, CDs and DVDs. Come see the wide variety of audio- and video material, a unique foreign language section, and children's play area. Call to get on the mailing list for a newsletter that lists special events such as author and illustrator talks and character appearances. Story times Mondays and Fridays at 10:30.

Noyes Library for Young Children

10237 Carroll Place
Kensington MD 20895
www6.montgomerycountymd.gov/Apps/Libraries/branchinfo/no.asp
240.773.9570

This charming one-room library, Montgomery County's oldest, is now an historic landmark. It sits on its own triangular island surrounded by old trees and turreted Victorian homes. Once inside, children immediately sense the intimacy of this library, which is just for them. The Library offers programs for babies, toddlers and preschoolers, as well as other special events. Adults can borrow special Grandparents Kits with books, toys, and media centered on a particular theme to have on hand for visiting youngsters. Open regularly on Tuesdays, Thursdays and Saturdays. Also open on select Wednesdays for story time programs, for which preregistration is required.

Politics and Prose

5015 Connecticut Ave NW
Washington DC 20008
www.politics-prose.com
202.364.1919
Metrorail Red line (Van Ness)

This independent, community-oriented bookstore is beloved and renowned for its stellar selection, knowledgeable staff and unparalleled author events. They feature frequent author talks, story hours, receptions for local authors, teen book clubs and other events. Try a Book of the Month club program, with books specially selected for your child!

Second Story Books

Rockville location:
12160 Parklawn Drive
Rockville MD 20852
301.770.0477
Metrorail Red line (Twinbrook)

DC location:
2000 P Street NW
Washington DC 20036
202.659.8884
Metrorail Red line (Dupont Circle)
www.secondstorybooks.com

Second Story Books has locations in Rockville and DC and carries a large selection of used, rare, and out-of-print books. Audio/visual material are also available. Stock varies greatly but there are always gems to be found, if you don't mind digging through the sometimes-disorganized inventory characteristic of used bookstores. Many wonderful children's books are out of print and only available at used bookstores or on Internet search services. Second Story Books can help you obtain titles that are out of print.

Sullivan's Toy Store

4200 Wisconsin Avenue NW
Washington DC 20016
202.362.1343
Metrorail Red line (Tenleytown)

This store has packed a lot of toys in a small space. There are toy, book, and art sections as well as party items. The book section is aimed primarily at very young children and features boards, pictures, books, activity and travel books and math and reading workbooks. Children will enjoy playing with the Brio train table while their parents shop. Family-owned (by the same family since it was founded), Sullivan's was the first store to carry the first edition of *Going Places With Children in Washington, DC* in 1958!

Toy Castle

Cabin John Shopping Center
11325 Seven Locks Road
Potomac MD 20854
www.toycastlepotomac.com
301.299.0680

A reincarnation of the owners' original store, toys... etc., this shop takes pride in selecting toys that encourage curiosity, creativity, and imagination. Located in Cabin John Shopping Center. Sister store to Toy Kingdom.

Toy Kingdom

36 Maryland Avenue
Rockville MD 20850
www.toykingdomllc.com
301.251.0220
Metrorail Red line (Rockville)

Just the right size for any toy store: large enough to have an excellent and well-chosen selection of toys, cards, books, and games, and small enough to feel welcoming and friendly. The staff is approachable and helpful. Sister store to Toy Castle.

Skating, Boarding and Blading

Bowie Skate Park

3330 Northview Drive
Bowie MD 20716
www.cityofbowie.org/Facilities.aspx?Page=detail&RID=11
301.809.3011

The Bowie Skate Park is a 10,000 square foot concrete skating facility that is open for skateboard and inline skating and offers both street and vert skating elements. The use of bicycles at this facility is not permitted. The facility is designed to challenge all skill levels and abilities. A helmet with chinstrap is required. The street course offers numerous skating elements including rolled banks, pump bumps, kinked rails, steps, quarterpipes, and a unique snake run that connects the bowl deck to the street course. For vert skaters, the bowl varies in depth from four to nine feet and sports an over vertical cradle that will challenge the most advanced skaters. Facility is non-staffed. Park design, photos and video available on website.

Cabin John Ice Rink

10610 Westlake Drive
Rockville MD 20852
www.montgomeryparks.org/enterprise/ice/cabin_john
301.765.8620

Cabin John Ice Rink has two large rinks and one small rink, and offers public skating hours, group and private lessons for all ages in figure skating and hockey, private party rentals and special themed skating events. Additional amenities include Pro Shop, cafe and free wifi. As of 2013, lessons follow the Basic Skills Curriculum under US Figure Skating. This state-of-the-art facility is open year round and has free and convenient parking.

Fairfax Ice Arena

3779 Pickett Road
Fairfax VA 22031
www.fairfaxicearena.com
703.323.1131

Fairfax Ice Arena has year-round public skating, offering lessons for children age four and older as well as adults. Additionally, the rink offers adult hockey leagues, summer camp programs, party packages, and assistance in organizing fundraisers for schools, churches and community groups. Other amenities include a Pro Shop, cafe and arcade games.

Fort Dupont Ice Arena

3779 Ely Place
Washington DC 20019
www.fdia.org
202.584.5007

The only public indoor ice arena in Washington, DC, the Fort Dupont Ice Arena offers public skating, lessons and individual or group competitive opportunities in figure skating, hockey, and speed skating. Facilities include educational meeting rooms with computer workstations, a pro shop and concession stand. The Friends of Fort Dupont Ice Arena founded Kids On Ice, a program that provides free or subsidized skating programs to children.

Gaithersburg Skate Park

510 S Frederick Avenue
Gaithersburg MD 20877
www.gaithersburgmd.gov/about-gaithersburg/city-facilities/skate-park
301.258.6539

Gaithersburg's 12,300 square foot skate park is designed for skateboards, inline skates, and BMX bikes. The park includes ramps and structures suitable for a wide range of skill levels. Some obstacles include an A-frame ramp and rail, mini-half pipe, 7-6' escalator, stairs, pyramid wedge, fun boxes, wall ride, and several quarters and banks of varying heights. All ramps are constructed with a wood frame and Skatelite surface. The ground is newly refurbished with an ultra-smooth acrylic paint allowing for even speed from ground to ramps. Other amenities include vending machines, coin-operated lockers, helmet/pad rentals, and an outdoor stereo system. Helmets are required for all skaters/bikers, and in-line skaters must also wear wrist guards. Elbow and knee pads are recommended, but not required. Children under the age of 8 must be accompanied by an adult.

Gardens Ice House

13800 Old Gunpowder Road
Laurel MD 20707
www.thegardensicehouse.pointstreaksites.com
301.953.0100

The Gardens is a state of the art recreational facility offering year-round skating on an Olympic size rink and two NHL-sized ice rinks in addition to seasonal skating on a connected outdoor rink. A wide range of activities and lessons are offered for all ages and skill levels in hockey, roller hockey, figure skating, speed skating, in-line skating, ice dancing, broomball, curling, and public open hours. Also available are summer camps, special programs for groups and fundraisers, birthday party packages, and a Zamboni driving school. Additional amenities include a Pro Shop, café and conference/event/banquet rooms, a library, and skating museum. The location also houses a Wellness for Life Fitness Center.

Herbert W. Wells Ice Rink

5211 Paint Branch Parkway
College Park MD 20740
www.pgparks.com/Things_To_Do/Sports/Ice_Skating/Herbert_Wells_
Ice_Rink.htm
301.277.3717
Metrorail Green and Yellow lines (College Park)

Open for ice-skating from October through March, this rink is used for roller skating and/or street hockey during the summer. The facility offers lessons for all ages and team activities in figure skating and ice hockey as well as birthday parties and field trip opportunities. No public skating hours.

Kettler Capitals IcePlex

627 N Glebe Road, Suite 800
Arlington VA 22203
www.kettlercapitalsiceplex.com
571.224.0555
Metrorail Orange line (Ballston)

Kettler Capitals IcePlex is a 20,000 square foot training center
for the Washington Capitals. The IcePlex features two indoor
NHL-sized ice rinks, office space, locker rooms, a full-service
ProShop, a Capitals Team Store, a snack bar, and space for
special events. Kettler offers public skating, as well as lessons
and programs in figure skating and hockey for all ages.
Washington Capitals practices are held at Kettler and are open
to the public and free of charge. The IcePlex is located atop the
Ballston Common Mall Parking Garage in Arlington, Virginia.

Mount Vernon Ice Arena

2017 Belle View Boulevard
Alexandria VA 22307
www.fairfaxcounty.gov/parks/rec/mv/mv-ice.htm
703.768.3224

This indoor NHL-sized ice arena is designed for year-round use
and offers public skating, figure skating, and hockey lessons for
all ages and abilities. Other activities include youth and adult
hockey leagues, pick-up hockey sessions, themed sessions for
figure skating enthusiasts, and birthday parties.

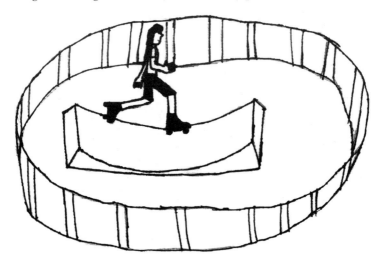

Olney Manor Skate Park

6601 Georgia Avenue
Olney MD 20832
www.montgomeryparks.org/parks_facilities_directory/olneymanorrp_
skate.shtm
301.905.3095

Olney Manor Skate Park offers 14,400 square-feet of skating
space featuring a 10-foot-deep bowl, Hubba ledge, steps with
handrail, quarter pipes, Fun Box with flat rail, manual pad,
and Pyramid Ledge. Open to skaters (skateboard and inline)
of all skill levels, age four and up though skaters age eight and
younger must be accompanied by a parent or guardian. In
addition to skating hours, the park also offers beginner skating
lessons, board and inline summer camps, and private rentals.

Reston Ice Skating Pavilion

1818 Discovery Street
Reston VA 20190
www.restontowncenter.com/skating
703.709.6300

The Reston Pavilion is located in the middle of Reston Town
Center and surrounded by restaurants, shops and a movie theater.
November thought March the Pavilion floor is transformed into
an ice skating rink. Ice skates and other supplies are available
inside the Skate Shop directly beside the Pavilion.

Rockville Ice Arena

50 Southlawn Court
Rockville MD 20850
www.rockvilleice.pointstreaksites.com
301.315.5650

This indoor, year-around ice skating facility, not far from
Rockville Town Center, houses three NHL-sized rinks. A wide
range of activities and lessons are offered for all ages and skill
levels including public skating, figure skating, hockey, speed
skating and broomball. The facility also houses a Pro Shop, an
electronic game arcade, and event rooms and offers birthday
parties. The adjacent Village Grille is a full service restaurant
capable of catering for skating related events.

Rockville Town Square Ice Rink

131 Gibbs Street
Rockville MD 20850
www.rockvilletownsquare.com/at-the-square/ice-rink
Metrorail Red line (Rockville)

This seasonal, outdoor rink is located in Rockville Town Square, surrounded by restaurants, shops, parking and other amenities such as the Rockville Town Library. The 7,200 square-foot rink offers public skating, figure skating lessons for all ages, beginner hockey lessons, birthday parties, corporate events, and private parties.

Rockville Skate Park at Welsh Park

355 Martins Lane
Rockville MD 20850
www.rockvillemd.gov/skatepark
240.314.8620

The City of Rockville Skate Park was built and renovated with input from local skaters and includes murals created and donated by local artists. Skate park features include a 24-foot wide, four-foot tall mini-ramp, a three-foot ton four-foot tall, 20-foot wide micro ramp with escalator and extension, one three-set and one five-set hubba ledges, a Euro-gap, a Pump-hump, Quarter pipes, rails, funboxes, and manual pads. It is an unsupervised and free park open from 9 a.m. until 10 p.m. daily. All skaters and free-style bikers are advised to wear a helmet, elbow pads, wrist guards, and kneepads. Classes are offered for beginning child skaters.

Sculpture Garden Ice-Skating Rink

9th Street between Constitution & Madison Avenues NW
Washington DC 20565
www.nga.gov/content/ngaweb/visit/ice-rink.html
202.216.9397
Metrorail Blue and Orange lines (Smithsonian), Green and Yellow lines (Archives-Penn Quarter-Navy Memorial), Red line (Judiciary Square)

The National Gallery of Art Sculpture Garden Ice Rink is open from mid-November through mid-March, weather permitting. View magnificent works of sculpture while skating in the open air and enjoying music from the state-of-the-art sound system.

Group and private ice-skating lessons are also available. The adjacent Pavilion Cafe sells food and drinks. Both the ice rink and cafe are open outside of museum hours.

Silver Spring Ice Skating at Veterans Arena

8523 Fenton Street
Silver Spring MD 20910
www.silverspringiceskating.com/iceskatingsilverspring.html
301.588.1221
Metrorail Red line (Silver Spring)

This seasonal outdoor rink is located in downtown Silver Spring on Veterans' Plaza and is surrounded by restaurants, shops and plenty of parking. The arena is also within walking distance from the Red Line/Silver Spring station. It offers public skating seven days a week, group lessons for all ages, private party rentals and ice skating birthday parties.

Skate-N-Fun Zone

7878 Sudley Road
Manassas VA 20109
www.skatenfunzone.com
703.361.7465

Skate-N-Fun offers in-line and roller-skating, as well as "Laser Storm," a laser tag game, a soft-play area, rock climbing wall and a video arcade. Roller skating lessons, private parties and group events are also available. A café and sweet shop are also on the premises.

SkateQuest

1800 Michael Faraday Court
Reston VA 20190
www.skatequest.com
703.709.1010

SkateQuest is a twin sheet indoor ice skating center with full service pro shop, café, and party rooms. Open year round, SkateQuest provides services for recreational skaters, figure skaters, and hockey players offering a wide range of lessons, camps, clinics and themed events for all ages and skill levels. Also available are off-ice conditioning, summer camps, special programs for groups and fundraisers and birthday party packages.

Tucker Road Ice Rink

1770 Tucker Road
Fort Washington MD 20744
www.pgparks.com/Things_To_Do/Sports/Ice_Skating/Tucker_Road_
Ice_Rink.htm
301.265.1525

This year-round indoor ice skating facility's amenities include a warming room, locker rooms, party room and spectator viewing room. Tucker Road Ice Rink also offers the following: public ice skating sessions with skate rentals, USFS Learn to Skate classes, Learn to Play Hockey classes, broom ball, summer day camps, ice and room rentals, birthday party packages and the very popular ice bumper cars.

Washington Harbour Ice Rink

3050 K Street NW
Washington DC 20007
www.thewashingtonharbour.com/skating
202.706.7666
Metrorail Blue and Orange (Foggy Bottom-GWU)

The 11,800 square foot Washington Harbour Ice Rink, located in the picturesque Georgetown neighborhood, is DC's largest outdoor ice skating venue and is open for public skating in mid-November through March and also offers skating classes, birthday party packages and private rentals.

Wheaton Ice Arena

11717 Orebaugh Avenue
Wheaton MD 20902
www.montgomeryparks.org/enterprise/ice/wheaton
301.905.3000

Open year-round, this NHL-sized rink offers sessions for all skating abilities and interests. Programs are offered for recreational, freestyle, hockey, and speed skaters. Also offered are a warming room, party rooms, pro shop, snack bar and workout facility, as well as themed skating events, fundraiser packages and Park Play Days when schools are closed for inclement weather.

Snowboarding and Skiing

Liberty Mountain Resort & Conference Center

78 Country Club Trail
Carrol Valley PA 17320
www.libertymountainresort.com
717.642.8282

Take a day trip to the slopes at Liberty Mountain Resort, located around 1.5 hours from DC. Liberty Mountain offers many different instructional choices for children and adults, from all day children's ski camps and childcare, to skiing, to snowboarding and snow tubing.

Roundtop Mountain Resort

925 Roundtop Road
Lewisberry PA 17339
www.skiroundtop.com
717.432.9631

Roundtop is primarily a ski and snowboard resort with 16 trails and 9 chair lifts, however snow tubing there is also popular. Instruction is available for all ages. In the summer, Roundtop offers paintball, ropes courses, vertical trekking, mountain adventure activities and summer camp.

Whitetail Resort

13805 Blairs Valley Road
Mercersburg PA 17236
www.skiwhitetail.com
717.328.9400

The Whitetail Resort, about 1.5 to 2 hours from DC, features skiing, snowboarding, and snow tubing on 108 acres of terrain with 17 trails, 6 lifts and a 935-foot vertical drop. Whitetail offers a variety of ski school programs for children as well as childcare and ski camp packages. In the spring, summer, and fall, Whitetail offers more than 30 miles of hiking trails, scenic chairlift rides, fly-fishing, and outdoor skills programs. There is also a summer Junior Adventure Camp program for children ages 12-16.

Wisp Resort

296 Marsh Hill Road
McHenry MD 21541
www.wispresort.com
301.387.4000

Wisp, about 3 hours from DC, is situated near Deep Creek Lake and offers 22 ski trails covering 100 acres of terrain. Winter activities include downhill and cross country skiing, snowboarding, snow tubing, snowshoeing, a mountain roller coaster, and kid-size mini-snowmobiles. Children's programs for ages 3-14 are available for half-and full-days and a Kids Night Out offers a drop-off opportunity for parents. The summer resort includes an 18-hole championship golf course, driving range, an Outdoor Adventures for kids ages 2 and up, a 20,000 square foot paved and wood skate park, paintball, scenic chairlift rides, a zip-line, mountain boarding and mountain biking. Sailboats are available for rent in the summer through mid-October.

Swimming and Splashing

Blue Planet SCUBA

1755 S Street NW
Washington DC 20009
www.blueplanetdc.com
202.527.9419
Metrorail Red line (Dupont Circle)

This scuba school focuses on providing the best education and travel experiences to divers in the Washington, DC area while harnessing the excitement and adventure of scuba to help protect our fragile oceans. Offers beginner, advanced, kids, and teen classes.

Bohrer Water Park at Summit Hall Farm

512 S Frederick Avenue
Gaithersburg MD 20877
www.gaithersburgmd.gov/about-gaithersburg/city-facilities/water-park-at-bohrer-park
301.258.6445

This park features a main pool with palm trees, two 250-foot water slides (one fast and one slower ride), floatable animals and a zero-depth entry for accessibility. For children under five, the splash pool features flume slides and a water-play structure. Also at the park are a playground, shaded areas, picnic tables, and snack bar. The nearby miniature golf course in a natural park setting has 18-holes. The park also has three putting greens, a children's playground, and a skate park. The Activity Center features two gymnasiums, three multi-purpose rooms, and fitness room.

Claude Moore Recreation Center

46105 Loudoun Park Lane
Sterling VA 20164
www.loudoun.gov/index.aspx?NID=1259
571.258.3600

This Loudon County Recreation Center offers a family-friendly leisure pool including a giant water slide, children's play area, hot tub, vortex, lazy river, and free swim and play area. Private swim lessons are also available in the adjacent Competitive Pool.

Downpour at Algonkian Regional Park

47001 Fairway Drive
Sterling VA 20165
www.nvrpa.org/park/downpour_at_algonkian/content/hours_and_ directions
703.450.4655

Downpour, the water playground at Algonkian Regional Park, is brimming with buckets of summertime water fun. A huge water bucket pours 800 gallons into the play pool every three minutes, drenching everyone in range. The bucket tops an intricate interactive tower in the play pool that invites children to climb, shoot water cannons, slide down one of two slides, and activate a variety of water jets. In the main pool, a 20-foot slide tower leads to two slides. Floating polyethylene-foam alligators and snakes, and a shipwreck slide add to the water fun in this free-form pool. Algonkian Regional Park offers a popular 18-hole championship golf course, a meeting and reception complex, 12 vacation cottages, group and family picnicking, boat launching, fishing, miniature golf and a nature trail. See Algonkian Regional Park, on page 79 for additional information.

Kennedy Shriver Aquatic Center

5900 Executive Boulevard
North Bethesda MD 20852
www6.montgomerycountymd.gov/rectmpl.asp?url=/content/rec/ thingstodo/aquatics/montgomery.asp
240.777.8070
Metrorail Red line (White Flint)

This accessible facility has a 50-meter, L-shaped indoor swimming pool. For divers there are one- and three-meter springboards and an 18-foot diving well. For an exciting thrill, children and parents will enjoy the 233-foot water slide. For younger children, there is a shallow pool with a beach-style entry featuring a waterfall. Group and private swimming lessons are also available.

Germantown Indoor Swim Center

18000 Central Park Circle
Boyds MD 20841
www6.montgomerycountymd.gov/rectmpl.asp?url=/content/rec/
thingstodo/aquatics/germantown.asp
240.777.6830

This fully accessible facility is approximately 60,000 square feet. The pools offer competition, recreation, leisure and two separate hydrotherapy pools, as well as diving platforms and a water slide. Swimming lessons, swim teams, dive teams, masters swimming, and scuba are available.

Lane Manor Splash Park

7601 West Park Drive
Hyattsville, MD 20783
www.pgparks.com/Things_To_Do/Sports/Aquatics/Lane_Manor_
Splash_Park.htm
301.422.7284 (Summer)
301.894.1150 (General Inquiries)

Located at Lane Manor Community Recreation Center, a 40-acre park within Northwest Branch Stream Valley Park, this seasonal, outdoor family splash park's amenities include a 25-meter pool, lily pad crossing feature, mushroom waterfall, water slides, children's wading pool, and shower/changing facilities. This facility offers American Red Cross swimming lessons and birthday parties are available by reservation.

Martin Luther King, Jr. Swim Center

1201 Jackson Road
Silver Spring MD 20904
www6.montgomerycountymd.gov/rectmpl.asp?url=/content/rec/
thingstodo/aquatics/martin.asp
240.777.8060

This swim center includes an eight-lane 25-meter stretch pool with a movable bulkhead, allowing for a separate diving area, diving boards and a five-meter platform, a Teach Pool for children and a hydrotherapy pool and is completely handicapped accessible. Times are available for lap swimming, recreational swimming, water fitness classes, swimming lessons, kayaking, lifeguard training, water safety, lifeguard instructor courses, CPR, and more.

Olney Indoor Swim Center

16605 Georgia Avenue
Olney MD 20904
www6.montgomerycountymd.gov/rectmpl.asp?url=/content/rec/
thingstodo/aquatics/olney.asp
240.777.4995

The Olney Swim Center offers many enticing features for children such as "Tumble Buckets," a waterfall mushroom, kiddie slides, and a beach-style entry. There are two hydrotherapy pools for adults, an 8-lane, 25-yard pool with separate diving areas for 1 and 3 meter boards. There is a sauna in each locker room, and a special dressing/locker room area for families or people with special needs. Times available for lap swimming, recreational swimming, water fitness classes, swimming lessons, water safety, lifeguard instructor courses, CPR, and more. Swim team, dive team and masters swimming are available.

Montgomery County Recreation Outdoor Pools MD

www6.montgomerycountymd.gov/rectmpl.asp?url=/content/rec/
thingstodo/aquatics/outdoor.asp

Montgomery County has seven seasonally available outdoor pools open to the public. All offer main pools, Tot Pools, and swimming lessons. Most offer Teach Pools, snack bars, and picnic areas. Some offer water-park style activities such as slides and other water-play features. Locations are in Bethesda, Germantown, Gaithersburg, Poolesville, Wheaton/Glenmont, and two locations in Silver Spring. Visit the website for the address, telephone number and description of each pool.

Rockville Municipal Swim Center

355 Martins Lane
Rockville MD 20850
www.rockvillemd.gov/swimcenter
240.314.8750

The Rockville Swim Center has two indoor and two outdoor
pools (one with a water slide and "beach"), a tot pool with
fountains, a new "sprayground," and exercise rooms.

Rollingcrest-Chillum Splash Pool

6122 Sargent Road
Chillum MD 20782
www.pgparks.com/Things_To_Do/Sports/Aquatics/Rollingcrest-
Chillum_Splash_Pool.htm
301.853.9115

Open year-round, Rollingcrest-Chillum Splash Pool offers
aquatics opportunities for people of all ages and swimming
abilities. The indoor pool facility includes: a heated, 20-yard
lap pool with a drop slide and lily pad walk; a heated family
pool with beach grade entry, a tube slide, otter slide, and water
play features; a heated whirlpool; a heated children's pool with
beach grade entry, waterplay features and fun slides; a lobby
observation area; locker rooms with coin-operated lockers;
and a family changing room. Also available are swimming
lessons, water aerobics, certification courses and birthday party
packages (available by reservation).

South Germantown Recreational Park Splash Playground and Miniature Golf

18056 Central Park Circle
Boyds MD 20841
www.montgomeryparks.org/enterprise/park_facilities/south_
germantown/splashplayground_minigolf.shtm
301.670.4680

South Germantown Recreational Park's Splash Playground has
a one-of-a-kind 280-jet water maze, cave with a waterfall, water
bucket drops, slide, and spraying animals. Tables and umbrellas
provide shaded rest areas. Restrooms, changing rooms with
lockers, and vending machines available onsite. Birthday party
packages and private event rentals are available. The park has one
18-hole Miniature Golf course adjacent to the Splash Playground.

Splash Down Water Park

7500 Ben Lomond Park Drive
Manassas VA 20109
www.splashdownwaterpark.com
703.361.4451

Splash Down Water Park offers 13 acres of fun with five unique water attraction areas, a shallow-entry beach area, water slides for all ages and thrill levels, water raindrops and bubblers, a 770-foot lazy river, special children's area, and more. Other amenities include playground, volleyball, tennis courts and a variety of pavilions. Three food venues offer the treats of summer, and catering services are offered.

Volcano Island Water Park

47001 Fairway Drive
Sterling VA 20164
www.volcanoislandwaterpark.com/features-attractions
703.430.7683

Located within Algonkian Regional Park (see page 79), Volcano Island is loaded with fun features for adults and kids. Volcano Island includes a 500-gallon dumping bucket, waterfalls, squirters and waterslides that offer a trio of riveting rides, including 230 feet of fun on the open slide, a thrilling 170 foot ride in complete darkness and a fast, quick ride on the tree stump slide. Other features are a Splash Pad, a Neo game, aquatics classes, group packages and birthday parties, and the Paradise Cafe.

Water Mine Family Swimmin' Hole

1400 Lake Fairfax Drive
Reston VA 20190
www.fairfaxcounty.gov/parks/rec/watermine
703.471.5415

Located in Lake Fairfax Park, this "old west" themed outdoor swimming facility offers more than an acre of water slides and interactive play features. While the main attractions are generally designed for elementary-aged children, there's something here for everyone. There are pint-sized slides and gentle bubblers for toddlers, and everyone can go with the flow in a tube on the lazy Rattlesnake River that circles the facility. Large tent and Funbrella rentals are also available.

Washington DC Indoor/Outdoor Pools

Here is a list of indoor and outdoor pools in Washington, DC. For more information on any of these locations please visit The District of Columbia Parks and Recreation website at www.app.dpr.dc.gov/dprmap

Anacostia Pool	Kelly Miller Pool
Banneker Pool	Langdon Park Pool
Benning Park Pool	Marie Reed Aquatic Center
Deanwood Aquatic Center	Oxon Run Pool
Douglass Pool	Randall Pool
Dunbar Aquatic Center	Rosedale Pool
East Potomac Pool	Takoma Aquatic Center
Ferebee-Hope Aquatic Center	Theodore Hagan Pool
Fort Dupont Pool	Turkey Thicket Aquatic Center
Fort Stanton Pool	Upshur Pool
Francis Pool	Volta Park Pool
Harry Thomas Sr. Recreation Center	William H. Rumsey Aquatic Center
Jelleff Recreation Center Pool	Wilson Aquatic Center

Virginia Indoor/Outdoor Pools

Great Waves Water Park	Alexandria VA
Paramount's Kings Dominion Water Works	Doswell VA
Atlantis Water Park at Bull Run Regional Park	Centreville VA
Great Waves at Cameron Run	Alexandria VA
Signal Bay Water Park	Manassas VA
Pirate's Cove Water Park at Pohick Bay	Lorton VA

Prince Georges County Indoor/Outdoor Pools

Six Flags: Hurricane Harbor	Mitchelville MD
Chesapeake Beach Water Park	Chesapeake Beach MD
Allentown Splash, Tennis & Fitness Club	Fort Washington MD
Ellen E Linson Splash Park	College Park MD
Glenn Dale Splash Park	Glenn Dale MD
Hamilton Splash Park	Hyattsville MD
North Barnaby Splash Park	Oxen Hill MD
Theresa Banks Memorial Aquatics Center	Glenarden MD
Fairland Sports & Aquatic Complex	Laurel MD

Indoor Recreation

BOWLING

Bowlmor Lanes

5353 Westbard Avenue
Bethesda MD 20816
www.bowlmor.com/bethesda
301.625.0955

15720 Shady Grove Road
Gaithersburg MD 20877
www.bowlmor.com/rockville
301.948.1390

You can't have a bad time there bowling!
HOLDEN, AGE 10

Bowl America Gaithersburg

1101 Clopper Road
Gaithersburg MD 20878
www.bowl-america.com
301.330.5200

White Oak Duckpin Bowling Lanes

11207 New Hampshire Avenue
Silver Spring MD 20904
www.whiteoaklanes.com
301.593.3000

INDOOR PLAY

The Autobahn Indoor Speedway

8251 Preston Court
Jessup MD 20794
www.autobahnspeed.com
410.880.0010

Experience European style indoor go-karting at a 70,000-square foot state-of-the-art facility in Howard County. Kids (once they reach 48 inches!) can race in karts designed just for them, reaching speeds of up to 25 mph! This is a great way for children to have their very first racing experience, and learn the fundamentals of friendly competition.

> *It's really, really fun! The go karts go around at least 60 miles per hour and they are all electric. It's indoors and you have to be eight years old to drive the karts.*
>
> SAMMY, AGE 8

Dynamite Gym

4956 Boiling Brook Parkway
North Bethesda MD 20852
www.dynamitegc.com
301.770.2700

A state-of-the-art gymnastics facility that offers classes for a variety of age groups, as well as birthday parties and Open Gym.

Funfit's Organically Grown Gym

1912 Olney Sandy Spring Road
Sandy Spring MD 20860
www.oggym.com
301.975.0099

A gym designed for both children and their parents, Funfit features kids' exercise bikes, hula-hoops, jump ropes, balls and other equipment for cardiovascular and strength exercise. Younger children can climb on soft wedges or jump in the moon bounce. Parents get a night out with a 'Just for Kids' party on the second Friday of every month.

Hill's Gymnastic Training Center

7557 Lindbergh Drive
Gaithersburg MD 20879
www.hillsgymnastics.com
301.840.5900

Olympic winners including Dominique Dawes have trained at Hill's, which features an open gym in addition to classes.

JW Tumbles

2499 N. Harrison Street
Arlington VA 22207
www.arlington.jwtumbles.com/find-us
703.531.1470

A place where kids can run, jump, climb, and tumble, JW Tumbles is an indoor gym that also offers classes and a Friday-night "Kids' Night Out" so parents can get a night on their own.

The Little Gym

1386 Lamberton Drive
Silver Spring MD 20902
www.tlgofsilverspringmd.com
301.681.7005

1071 Seven Locks Road
Potomac Woods Plaza
Potomac, MD 20854
www.tlgpotomacmd.com
301.294.4890

The Little Gym provides class for children ages four months to 12 years old in dance, gymnastics, sports skills, and karate. The gyms also host birthday parties and parent's night out for members. All classes are divided into themed, multi-week "learning units." Check website for class descriptions, and availability.

Marvatots 'n' Teens

5636 Randolph Road
Rockville MD 20852
www.marvatotsnteens.com
301.468.9181

Do somersaults, bounce on the trampoline, or try the bars at this gymnastic center. Offers classes for toddlers through teenagers.

My Gym

11325 Seven Locks Road
Potomac MD 20854
www.mygym.com/potomac
301.983.5300

Swings, slides, balls, and climbing apparatus for babies six weeks to age 13. Also featuring classes in music, dance and gymnastics. In the Cabin John Shopping Center.

Parent Resource Centers

332 West Edmonston Drive
Rockville MD 20853
www.mcitpfamilysupportnetwork.ning.com/events/parent-resource-centers
301.279.8497

The Parent Resource Centers provide a classroom-like setting for parents and children to play and learn together with the guidance of a parent educator. The centers have preschool toys, books, games and art activities; they also provide help with problem-solving for parents and a chance to share ideas and concerns.

INDOOR CLIMBING

Dick's Sporting Goods

2 Grand Corner Avenue
Gaithersburg MD 20878
www.dickssportinggoods.com
301.947.0200

Dick's offers one climbing wall within its retail store. A Dick's staffer serves as belayer while kids climb. A parent or guardian must be present during the climbing.

Earth Treks Climbing Center

725 Rockville Pike
Rockville MD 20852
www.earthtreksclimbing.com
240.283.9942

Earth Treks Climbing Center is an indoor climbing gym
with 44-foot high walls and more than 15,000 square feet of
climbing surfaces. Extensive hours and programs for beginning
and experienced climbers. Climbers younger than 14 must be
accompanied by an adult unless otherwise noted.

Sportrock Climbing Center

5308 Eisenhower Avenue
Alexandria VA 22304
www.sportrock.com/facilities/alexandria
703.212.7625
Metrorail Blue line (Van Dorn Street)

Sportrock Climbing Center is an indoor rock climbing facility
that provides instruction for children, teens, and adults. In
addition to birthday parties and summer camps, it offers a variety
of programs. On Friday evenings, children ages 6-13 can take
part in Kid's Night, which introduces them to general principles
of climbing and includes 1.5 hours of climbing time (similar
one-hour sessions are available on weekends). Older children
can take part in a basic skills course and then join a junior
climbing club on Thursday evenings which provides instruction
in movement, technical skills, and ropes management. Fees vary;
call for details. Participants must pre-register and pre-pay, as
well as sign liability waivers. This is a safe, fun, and controlled
environment for children to experience rock climbing.

MAKE-YOUR-OWN ART STUDIOS

All Fired Up

4923 Elm Street
Bethesda MD 20814
www.allfiredupdc.com
301.654.3206

At All Fired Up, you can create a mosaic with colored tiles,
returning 24 hours later to grout the tiles and take your creation
home. (The store will grout for you for additional fee.)

Clay Café Studio

101 N Maple Avenue
Falls Church VA 22046
www.claywire.com
703.534.7600

Select a ceramic piece, have fun painting it, and then pick up
your glazed and fired piece about four days later.

Color Me Mine

823 Ellsworth Drive
Silver Spring MD 20910
www.silverspring.colormemine.com
301.565.5105

The Mud Hut

3231 Spartan Road
Olney MD 20832
www.mudhutstudios.com
301.260.8786

Paint Your Own Pottery

10417 Main Street
Fairfax VA 22030
www.ciao-susanna.com/home.php
703.218.2881

Select from a huge array of stencils, stamps and idea books, or
create your own designs.

LASER TAG AND ARCADES

LaserNation/UltraZone

3447 Carlin Springs Road
Bailey's Crossroads VA 22041
www.ultralasertag.com
703.578.6000

Laser Quest

14517 Potomac Mills Circle
Woodbridge VA 22193
www.laserquest.com
703.490.4180

Shadowland

624 Quince Orchard Road
Gaithersburg MD 20878
www.shadowlandadventures.com
301.330.5546

XP Laser Sport

14705 Baltimore Avenue
Laurel MD 20707
www.xplasersport.com
301.953.2266 or 410.833.6611

SWEET TREATS

After a day of adventures in the Washington, DC area, sometimes you just want a sweet treat. Many neighborhoods are home to terrific cupcakes, ice cream, and chocolates. A few of our favorites:

BAKERIES
Georgetown Cupcake

3301 M Street NW
Washington DC 20007
202.333.8448

4834 Bethesda Avenue
Bethesda MD 20814
301.907.8900
www.georgetowncupcake.com

Hello Cupcake

1361 Connecticut Avenue NW
Washington DC 20036
www.hellocupcakeonline.com
202.861.2253

Pie Sisters

3423 M Street NW
Washington DC 20007
www.piesisters.com
202.338.7437

Sweet Lobby

404 8th Street SE
Washington DC 20003
www.sweetlobby.com
202.544.2404

ICE CREAM
Thomas Sweet

3214 P Street NW
Washington DC 20007
www.thomassweet.com
202.337.0616

Dolcezza Artisanal Gelato

1704 Connecticut Avenue NW
Washington DC 20009
202.299.9116

1560 Wisconsin Avenue NW
Washington DC 20007
202.333.0933

1418 14th Street NW
Washington DC 20005
202.817.3900

7111 Bethesda Lane
Bethesda MD 20814
301.215.9226

2905 District Avenue
Fairfax VA 22031
703.992.8701
www.dolcezzagelato.com

CHOCOLATES
Artisan Confections

1025 N. Fillmore Street
Arlington VA 22201
703.524.0007

2910 District Avenue
Fairfax VA 22031
703.992.6130
www.artisanconfections.com

Max Brenner

7263 Woodmont Avenue
Bethesda MD 20814
301.215.8305
www.maxbrenner.com/locations/usa/restaurant-bethesda

Chocolate Chocolate

1130 Connecticut Avenue
Washington DC 20036
www.chocolatedc.com
202.466.2190

Did we miss your favorite?
Tell us at: GoingPlaces@greenacres.org for possible inclusion in a
future edition of *Going Places*.

Day Trips

The Washington, DC area is surrounded by fun and exciting places that make great day trips—natural wonders like the Chesapeake Bay and the Shenandoah and Allegheny mountains; significant sites from Civil War and Colonial history; fascinating cities and charming small towns.

With so many potential trips, we've stuck fairly close to home—within about a two hours drive. We have provided a few of our favorites and provided references for you to search farther afield.

ANNAPOLIS

Banneker-Douglass Museum

84 Franklin Street
Annapolis MD 21401
www.bdmuseum.com
410.216.6180

Named for scientist and inventor Benjamin Banneker and abolitionist Frederick Douglass, this museum is dedicated to preserving Maryland's African American history. Housed in the old Mount Moriah A.M.E. Church, this museum includes art, photography, rare books and documents illustrating the role of African-Americans in Maryland history.

The Chesapeake Children's Museum

25 Silopanna Road
Annapolis MD 21403
www.theccm.org
410.990.1993

The Chesapeake Children's Museum offers a hands-on experience for children of all ages—but is especially appropriate for preschool and early elementary age children. The mission of the museum "is to create an environment of discovery about oneself, the peoples, the technologies, and the ecology of the Chesapeake Bay area for all our children and for the children in us all."

Highlights include a "Bay Window" exhibit of live aquatic and land-dwelling animals, the seven-foot-tall human replica "Stuffee," which can be taken apart to see the internal organs, and a stage with dress-up costumes and audience seating for impromptu performances. An art and science workshop space is available for exploration by reservation. The museum's new facility provides outdoor areas including an herb garden and the Harriet Tubman Walk—a simulated walk along the Underground Railroad.

Historic Annapolis Foundation Welcome Center and Museum Store

18 Pinkey Street
Annapolis MD 21401
www.annapolis.org
410.267.7619

Housed in the old Victualling Warehouse, this museum offers an interesting diorama of the port of Annapolis as it was 200 years ago, when Annapolis was the principal seaport of the Upper Chesapeake Bay.

Pirate Adventures on the Chesapeake

311 Third Street
Annapolis MD 21403
www.chesapeakepirates.com
410.263.0002

Climb aboard this pirate ship for a family friendly adventure. Your child will be transformed into a pirate or mermaid with costumes and makeup and will get caught up in this real life adventure. The crew members guide the pirates through a treasure hunt that involves a treasure map, "stinky" Pirate Pete, and heavy use of water cannons. This is a great afternoon on the Chesapeake. The cruises run seven days a week in the summer and on the weekends through October. Check the website for details on sailing times, dates, ticket prices, and directions.

Quiet Waters Park

600 Quiet Waters Park Road
Annapolis MD 21403
www.aacounty.org/recparks/parks/quietwaters
410.222.1777

Scenically located on the South River and Harness Creek near Annapolis, this 336-acre park offers natural beauty and a variety of recreational activities. The park has over six miles of hiking/biking trails, six picnic pavilions available by reservation, open picnic areas (some with grills), scenic South River overlook, formal gardens, a large children's playground, and a cafe. Visitors can rent bicycles, sailboats, pedal boats, rowboats, kayaks, and canoes. There is an outdoor ice skating rink open from November through March. Two art galleries are located in the Visitor's Center. Juried sculpture from across the country is displayed throughout the park as part of the Sculpture in the Park program.

Sandy Point State Park

1100 E College Parkway
Annapolis MD 21409
www.dnr.state.md.us/publiclands/southern/sandypoint.asp
410.974.2149

Swim, fish, hike, boat, bird-watch, and picnic on this 786-acre park and beach at the foot of the eastern side of the Bay Bridge. Watch sailboats and freighters on the Bay. Or enjoy the playgrounds, marinas and cross-country skiing in winter.

State House Visitor Center

100 State Circle
Annapolis MD 21401
www.msa.maryland.gov/msa/mdstatehouse/html/home.html
410.946.5400

The State House is the oldest State Capitol in continuous legislative use. On the first floor is the Old Senate Chamber where George Washington resigned his commission as Commander-in Chief before the Continental Congress on December 23, 1783. The State House in Annapolis was the first peacetime Capitol, from November 1783 to August 1784. Maryland Legislature meets for 90 days, second Wednesday in January to April. Maryland school groups can arrange meetings with members of their county's senators or delegates during this time.

U.S. Naval Academy

121 Blake Road
Annapolis MD 21402
www.usna.edu
410.293.1000

This is the part of Annapolis that many youngsters really want to see. Favorites are the Armel-Leftwich Visitor Center and U.S. Naval Academy museum, the crypt of John Paul Jones, and the statue of Tecumseh. The Rogers Ship Model Collection contains 108 ship models dating from 1650-1850, and includes models of British Ships constructed by French prisoners of war during the Napoleonic conflict. At noon on some days, you may be lucky to see the midshipmen line up in front of Bancroft Hall and march with bugles and drums. Try not to visit during graduation (third week in May) because it is extremely crowded.

Watermark Cruises

1 Dock Street
Annapolis MD 21401
www.watermarkcruises.com
410.268.7601

Take advantage of this wonderful way to see such sights as the U.S. Naval Academy, Historic Annapolis Harbor, the scenic Severn River, the Chesapeake Bay, or even a trip to St. Michaels on the Eastern Shore of Maryland. Cruises depart from and return to the City Dock, located in the heart of historic downtown Annapolis. Various cruises are available, from 40 minutes to seven and 1/2 hours. Choose the cruise that's right for you!

William Paca House and Garden

186 Prince George Street
Annapolis MD 21401
www.annapolis.org/index.asp?pageid=49
410.990.4543

This 37-room, five-part mansion was built by William Paca, a signer of the Declaration of Independence and three-term governor of Maryland. The two-acre terraced garden behind the house, hidden for many years, was uncovered through archaeological excavation. The garden includes roses, boxwoods, flowerbeds, hollies, a Chinese trellis bridge, domed summer house, and fish-shaped pond.

BALTIMORE

American Visionary Art Museum

800 Key Highway
Baltimore MD 21230
www.avam.org
410.244.1900

This national museum and education center is dedicated to extraordinary works of art created by intuitive, self-taught artists, many regarded as eccentric in their passionate pursuit of artistic expression. The 55-foot tall whirligig is an eye-catcher even before you enter the museum; inside, there are six art galleries, a wild flower sculpture garden, museum store, and restaurant.

Babe Ruth Museum

216 Emory Street
Baltimore MD 21201
www.baberuthmuseum.org
410.727.1539

Here is an opportunity for fans of all ages to visit the house where baseball's number one slugger was born, and to view mementos and films of Babe Ruth. You will also get a feel for Maryland's baseball heritage and Orioles history. Exhibits change each year. Easily accessible from Camden Yards!

The Baltimore Civil War Museum/President Street Station

601 President Street
Baltimore MD 21202
www.civilwarbaltimore.com
410.878.6411

The museum tells the stories of Baltimore's role in the Civil War, especially the Pratt Street Riot which accounted for the first bloodshed of the War. The museum also explains the link between this railroad station and the Underground Railroad, as well as the story of the Philadelphia, Wilmington and Baltimore Railroads.

Baltimore and Ohio Railroad Museum

901 W Pratt Street
Baltimore MD 21223
www.borail.org
410.752.2490

This old roundhouse contains the world's largest collection of locomotives, cabooses, freights, and other cars dating back to 1829. Children can go through a caboose and the back of a mail car. The large model railroad station is always a hit. Enter the museum through Mt. Claire Station, the oldest railroad station in the United States.

Baltimore Maritime Museum

301 Pier 3
Baltimore MD 21202
www.historicships.org
410.539.1797

This is a great favorite for children. They always love the tours of these three vessels, even if they aren't old enough to understand the different naval technologies presented. The Taney is the last surviving warship from the attack of Pearl Harbor, and the Torsk sank the last two Japanese combatant ships of WWII. Lightship Chesapeake, a floating lighthouse, marked entrance ways to harbors when other navigational devices were impractical. The seven-foot Knoll Lighthouse marked the mouth of the Patapsco River for 133 years before being moved.

Baltimore Museum of Art

10 Art Museum Drive
Baltimore MD 21218
www.artbma.org
443.573.1700

This exceptional museum features the Cone Collection of early
20th century art. Matisse and Picasso are particularly well
represented. Children of all ages are invited to sample the colorful
palette of workshops, performances, and education programs
presented by the BMA. Each program is designed to educate and
fascinate by introducing young people to the world of art.

Baltimore Museum of Industry

1415 Key Highway
Baltimore MD 21230
www.thebmi.org
410.727.4808

Voted "Best Hands-On Museum for Kids" by *Baltimore Magazine*.
This hands-on museum, located in the heart of industrial south
Baltimore, contains a print shop, a machine shop, a garment
loft, and an assembly line where youngsters learn how parts
become finished products. This museum is a great "find."
Housed in a harbor-side cannery that was used during the Civil
War to send oysters off to the soldiers, the building itself bears
testimony to the working life the museum recreates.

Baltimore Streetcar Museum

1901 Falls Road
Baltimore MD 21211
www.baltimorestreetcar.org
410.547.0264

A rolling history of the streetcars of Baltimore, the museum
houses a collection of Baltimore streetcars, horse-drawn
and electric, covering the 104-year history of this type of
transportation in the city. Enjoy unlimited streetcar rides,
tours, exhibits, and a slide show in addition to a collection of
Baltimore streetcars from 1859-1963.

The Baltimore Zoo

1876 Mansion House Drive
Baltimore MD 21217
www.marylandzoo.org
410.396.7102

Rated as having the best children's zoo in the country by *The Zoo Book: A Guide to America's Best*, the Baltimore Zoo is home to over 2,200 exotic animals and wildlife. The Children's Zoo has 48 interactive exhibits where kids can experience what it is like to burrow underground like woodchucks or hop on a lily pad like a frog. Travel to the African Watering Hole, a spectacular six-acre home for zebras, pelicans, white rhinos, lions, cheetahs, extraordinary birds, and visit a habitat for African black-footed penguins, the Chimpanzee Forest, and the Leopard Lair!

Federal Hill Park

300 Warren Avenue
Baltimore MD 21230
www.baltimore.to/FederalHill
410.396.5828

Located in the heart of downtown Baltimore, historical Federal Hill Park offers a beautiful country setting with a picnic area and playground and an excellent view of the Inner Harbor!

Fire Museum

1301 York Road
Lutherville MD 21093
www.firemuseummd.org
410.321.7500

America's premier collection of fire-fighting apparatus awaits you at the Fire Museum. More than 40 fire engines are on display. See hand-pulled trucks that required forty to fifty men to pull them, horse-drawn trucks, and the motorized trucks of the 1950's. This museum helps children learn the history of fire fighting. Experience the thrill of sending an alarm over an antique fire alarm system, visit the dress-up corner where kids can put on fire fighter boots and turnaround coats, explore the Children's Discovery Room and shop in the Museum store.

Fort McHenry National Monument and Historic Shrine

2400 E Fort Avenue
Baltimore MD 21230
www.nps.gov/fomc
410.962.4290

From a ship in Baltimore's outer harbor, Francis Scott Key saw the Star-Spangled Banner still flying from the ramparts of Fort McHenry after a 25-hour bombardment by the British in the War of 1812, inspiring him to write the National Anthem. A movie at the Visitor Center explains about the battle and the writing of the national anthem. Children are interested in the cannons and enjoy the soldiers in period uniforms on summer weekends.

Harborplace and The Gallery

201 E Pratt Street
Baltimore MD 21202
www.harborplace.com
410.323.1000

Harborplace and The Gallery are located in the heart of Baltimore's financial and business district, overlooking its Inner Harbor. Its three main buildings offer an exciting range of more than 200 shops, restaurants, stalls, and harbor-side terraces, as well as easy access to several main attractions, such as the National Aquarium and the Maryland Science Center. You can take a ride in paddleboats or travel on the Water Taxi to the various sights on the Inner Harbor. The outdoor promenades are perfect for strolling, skipping, pushing a stroller, or people watching. In good weather, you may be lucky and run into street performers who will keep you and your children amused.

Ladew Topiary Gardens

3535 Jarrettsville Pike
Monkton MD 21111
www.ladewgardens.com
410.557.9570

Self-taught gardener Harvey Ladew created 15 garden "rooms"—each with its own theme—on part of his Maryland estate. His creation has been called "the most outstanding garden in America." A 1.5 mile nature walk leads through woods, fields and across a wetland board walk.

Lexington Market

400 W Lexington Street
Baltimore MD 21201
www.lexingtonmarket.com
410.685.6169

This world-famous market has been in operation since 1782 and is one of the oldest markets in the United States. Ralph Waldo Emerson referred to it as the "gastronomic capital of the universe." Over 130 merchants can be found selling food from all around the world. The market bustles and offers a multitude of sights, sounds, smells, and tastes. A great place to stop for lunch or a snack—you may sample food from a variety of food stalls.

Maryland Historical Society

201 W Monument Street
Baltimore MD 21201
www.mdhs.org
410.685.3750

Museum highlights include a Hands-On-History Room with a rope bed, cast iron cook stove, butter churns, try-on clothing and "A Child's world," featuring 300 years of toys and games. Dioramas trace Maryland history in the Darnall Young People's Museum. The original manuscript of the "Star-Spangled Banner" is housed here in an exhibit on the War of 1812. Another exhibit focuses on the history of the Civil War in Maryland.

Maryland Science Center

601 Light Street
Baltimore MD 21230
www.mdsci.org
410.685.2370

Lots of kid friendly scientific information.
ERIN, AGE 9

You can easily spend a whole day in this excellent museum with its permanent exhibits on energy, the Chesapeake Bay, space, structures, and the Hubble space telescope. Many hands-on exhibits will keep your children involved. Temporary exhibits change every three months, so it is a place you can visit often.

National Aquarium in Baltimore

501 E Pratt Street
Baltimore MD 21202
www.aqua.org
410.576.3800

The National Aquarium is a spectacular, seven-level structure that houses fascinating and sophisticated aquatic exhibits. Children especially like the children's cove where they can hold horseshoe crabs, sea stars, and other small animals. A favorite is the marine mammal pavilion. Watch bottlenose dolphins and their trainers! But be careful, you could get wet! In the surrounding education arcade, kids can learn humpback whale songs, create bubbles to help humpbacks engulf their meals, and play "Whales in Jeopardy." Be sure to visit the Exploration Station, Atlantic Coral Reef, large shark exhibits, and rain forest. A complete tour will take about two and a half hours.

The Aquarium is one of Baltimore's most popular attractions, so it is best to visit in late afternoon or evening to avoid the crowds. If you think your family will visit the Aquarium more than once a year, you may save money by becoming a member.

National Museum of Dentistry

31 S Greene Street
Baltimore MD 21201
www.dentalmuseum.org
410.706.0600

The Dr. Samuel D. Harris National Museum of Dentistry, an affiliate of the Smithsonian Institution, gives an educational overview of the history of dentistry and the importance of good oral care. This is done through exciting interactive exhibitions and the careful preservation and creative presentation of dental artifacts. Experience the amazing feats of an "iron jaw" performer, play a tune on the tooth jukebox, and view George Washington's "not-so-wooden" teeth.

Port Discovery Children's Museum

35 Market Place
Baltimore MD 21202
www.portdiscovery.org
410.864.2700

Port Discovery, designed in collaboration with Walt Disney Imagineering, offers three floors of interactive fun for the whole family. 80,000 square feet of interactive exhibits cater to children ages 6-12, although children of all ages will find something to spark their interest. The central core of the museum is a three-story climbing structure...why take the stairs when there's a more challenging way to the top floor? Each floor is filled with fabulously creative exhibits and hand-on activities. Try to find the missing family members of Miss Perception's Mystery House or star in a kid-geared game show; create and build a project to take home in the R&D Dream Lab or challenge yourself to a memory game of colors and lights.

Reginald F. Lewis Museum of Maryland African-American History and Culture

830 E Pratt Street
Baltimore MD 21202
www.rflewismuseum.org
443.263.1800

Opened to the public in 2005, this 82,000 square-foot facility provides permanent and changing exhibits on Maryland's rich African American history and culture, along with an oral history studio and interactive learning opportunities. The museum theater hosts dance and musical performances, film festivals and lectures.

Star-Spangled Banner Flag House

844 E Pratt Street
Baltimore MD 21202
www.flaghouse.org
410.837.1793

This is the home of Mary Pickersgill, the young woman who sewed the 30' x 42' flag that flew over Fort McHenry during the Battle of Baltimore. This is the flag that inspired Francis Scott Key to write our National Anthem. Step back to the early 1800's and learn how Mary and her family lived and worked. The house is furnished with antiques of the Federal period, and the adjacent 1812 Museum houses a collection of artifacts from the War of 1812 and features a video program where you will hear the stirring story of the Battle of Baltimore.

Sports Legends at Camden Yards

201 W Camden Street
Baltimore MD 21202
www.baberuthmuseum.org
410.727.1539

Fans of all sports will find something to love in this interactive sports museum. Kids can sit on the bench in a locker room and try on uniforms from the Frederick Keys, Baltimore Ravens and other teams in the Locker Room-Kids' Discovery Zone. See an array of products endorsed by the Babe from a 1930s fountain pen, to the first Babe Ruth Home Run chocolate bar, men's underwear and toys. Watch the moving video of Cal Ripken's "2131" and see the banner that was unfurled that day when he broke Lou Gehrig's record for the most consecutive games played.

U.S.S. Constellation

301 E Pratt Street
Baltimore MD 21202
www.historicships.org
410.539.1797

The U.S.S. Constellation is another guaranteed favorite for
kids. This 1854 ship-of-war was the last sailing ship of the U.S.
Navy. It is the oldest American warship and the only Civil War
era vessel still afloat. The U.S.S. Constellation has hands-on
activities and demonstrations for visitors as they explore life on
board and see how thousands of sailors lived at sea.

Walters Art Gallery

600 N Charles Street
Baltimore MD 21201
www.thewalters.org
410.547.9000

This gallery is considered one of America's great public museums,
with a collection that spans 5,000 years of artistic achievement,
ranging from its well-known ancient Egypt collection to the
French Impressionists. Children typically enjoy the collection
of arms and armor, as well as the Egyptian mummy exhibit.
The museum provides many hands-on workshops, concerts,
storytelling, and docent-led tours for children.

World Trade Center "Top of the World"

401 E Pratt Street
Baltimore MD 21202
www.viewbaltimore.org
410.837.1793

Get an aerial overview of Baltimore from the 27th floor of the
tallest pentagon-shaped building in the world. Here you'll find
spectacular 360-degree panoramic views of Baltimore along
with stationed binoculars and photo-map guides describing
the local attractions, significant landmarks (like the Bromo
Seltzer Tower, the world's largest four-dial gravity clock, and
Baltimore's only Art Deco skyscraper) plus views of Camden
Yards and a breathtaking view of the Inner Harbor.

CHESAPEAKE BAY/WESTERN MARYLAND

Breezy Point Beach

5300 Breezy Point Road
Chesapeake Beach MD 20732
www.co.cal.md.us/Facilities.aspx?Page=detail&RID=15
410.535.0259

Visit the Chesapeake Bay! Spend the day exploring the beach, swimming, fishing or picnicking in the shade. Spend the night at a bay-front campsite. Collect fossils and search for shark teeth!

Catoctin Wildlife Preserve and Zoo

13019 Catoctin Furnace Road
Thurmont MD 21788
www.cwpzoo.com
301.271.3180

Catoctin Wildlife Preserve and Zoo is a privately owned zoo that delivers fun, intimate, educational encounters with exotic animals. Covering 35 acres filled with natural wildlife, the zoo exhibits bears, boas, macaws, monkeys, big cats and small mammals in an up-close manner...perfect for children. Shows called "Encounters" are scheduled seasonally, where visitors can play with a baby animal, get the "bear facts" on grizzlies, rub and scrub the 575-pound tortoise, talk to a tiger, and hug a boa constrictor.

Calvert Marine Museum

14200 Solomons Island Road
Solomons MD 20688
www.calvertmarinemuseum.ticketforce.com
410.326.2042

Located at the confluence of the Patuxent River and the Chesapeake Bay, the Calvert Marine Museum offers a hands-on opportunity to learn about maritime history, paleontology, and the unusual biology of the estuary (when salt and fresh water mix). The museum has 15 tanks which display the amazing diversity of life found in the Chesapeake Bay and Patuxent River. There are boats, models, paintings, and woodcarvings that showcase the lives of watermen, cannery workers, and shipbuilders. Outside, river otters frolic in the water next to a salt marsh that is home to crabs, herons and egrets. Take a walk to the Drum Point Lighthouse, just behind the museum, that dates back to 1883. Another great way to experience the area is to board an old oyster boat built in 1899.

Chesapeake Beach Railway Museum

4155 Mears Avenue
Chesapeake Beach MD 20732
www.cbrm.org
410.257.3892

Chesapeake Beach was a popular resort destination for many years prior to World War II. This museum tells the history of the resort and of the railroad that connected it to DC and Baltimore from 1900 to the mid-1930s. Although there are no full-size trains to see, children will enjoy the model trains, photos from the early railroad days, and an old-fashioned toy locomotive. The museum is housed in a turn-of-the-century railroad station, the last surviving station of the Chesapeake Railroad. At the museum, visitors can see artifacts, photographs, a model of the early boardwalk, and share stories with old timers from the beach. One of the treasures of the museum is a stenciled kangaroo from a Dentzel carousel, as well as a 1914 Ford station wagon. That kangaroo and the carousel are now located at Watkins Regional Park in Prince George's County.

Chesapeake Beach Water Park

4079 Gordon Stinnett Ave
Chesapeake Beach MD 20732
www.chesapeakebeachwaterpark.com
410.257.1404

This water park is a great place to take a break from the heat and humidity of a Washington summer. Located at the Chesapeake Bay, this park offers eight water slides of varying thrill levels, including one that is wheelchair accessible. There is a separate pool for very little ones and a children's activity pool where kids can wrestle an alligator or swim with a giant serpent. Dreamland River, waterfalls, and fountains add to the fun! Parents with older kids can pass the time swimming laps or playing water volleyball. Families can also watch the action while relaxing in the beach area.

The Children's Museum of Rose Hill Manor Park

1611 N Market Street
Frederick MD 21701
www.rosehillmuseum.com
301.600.1650

This delightful children's museum is located on a 43-acre historic park. The staff prides itself on making the 19th century come to life for its visitors. Children and adults may participate in hands-on activities. Make sure you visit more than the manor house. Follow your child's interest to the carriage museum, blacksmith shop, log cabin, icehouse, and herb and flower gardens. Costumed interpreters conduct the tours and encourage children to make stitches on a quilt, card wool, grind herbs, operate toy banks, and more.

Deep Creek Lake State Park

Swanton MD 21561
www.dnr.state.md.us/publiclands
301.387.4111

Deep Creek Lake State Park and the surrounding resort areas are nestled into Maryland's beautiful western mountains, in the Alleghany Highlands. Deep Creek Lake, Maryland's largest, was the result of a 1920's hydroelectric project on Deep Creek. The area gets 100 to 200 feet of snow in winter, summer nights are cool, and the autumn foliage is impressive. Swimming, fishing, and picnicking are available along the shoreline in Deep Creek Lake State Park. Hiking and canoeing are available at Meadow Mountain and Meadow Mountain Cove in the park.

Flag Ponds Nature Park

1525 Flag Ponds Parkway
Lusby MD 20657
www.calvertparks.org/fpp.ftml
410.586.1477

A mile of sandy beach and excellent shark-tooth hunting await those willing to take the lovely but steep two-mile hike to the shore. Hike, swim, fish, picnic and view wildlife at this 327-acre park and beach. Visit the nature center and talk to staff about the ponds, swamps, freshwater marshes and cliffs that support the ecosystem.

Greenbrier State Park

21843 National Pike
Boonsboro MD 21713
www.dnr.state.md.us/publiclands/western/greenbrier.asp
301.791.4767

Greenbrier State Park is a 1,288-acre park ten miles east of
Hagerstown and less than an hour's drive from Washington.
The park's picnic area overlooks a 42-acre man-made lake, with
a swimming area marked off with buoys and ropes. The peaceful,
wooded setting makes this spot a nice swimming alternative to
the noisy neighborhood pool. A small sandy beach slopes up to
the tree-shaded picnic area, with picnic tables, barbecue grills and
a pleasant view of the water. There is a small concession stand
and a bathhouse with restrooms, changing rooms and showers.
You can fish from the pier and rent a rowboat or canoe. You
pay a day-use fee when you enter the park, allowing you access
to the beach as well as other areas. Campsites are available.

National Museum of Civil War Medicine

48 E Patrick Street
Frederick MD 21705
www.civilwarmed.org
301.695.1864

For Civil War buffs and children curious about medicine and
nursing, this unique museum offers a fascinating picture of
wartime health care over 100 years ago.

The museum is dedicated to telling the medical story of the
American Civil War. Photographs, drawings, and displays of
all kinds of Civil War-era medicine bring to life the treatment
available to soldiers. The museum may not be appropriate for
young children, but if you can call ahead at least two weeks,
the staff can tailor a tour that is age-appropriate for your
family or group.

In addition to the permanent exhibits, the museum has special
events scheduled each month. Some examples: living historians
portray nurses and doctors in period dress, a Union drummer boy
talks about the role of children in the Civil War, and an exhibit
of African-American contributions to Civil War medicine.

The museum is an official site on the Civil War Discovery Trail. You might want to combine this site with a visit to the Battleground at Antietam.

Rocky Gap State Park

12500 Pleasant Valley Road
Flintston MD 21530
www.dnr.state.md.us/publiclands/western/rockygap.asp
301.722.1480

A beautiful place to vacation, Rocky Gap State Park features a 243-acre lake surrounded by mountains, and inexpensive lodgings at the 220-room lakeside lodge, Rocky Gap Lodge and Golf Resort. Take a swim in the lake, rent canoes, go fishing, and enjoy the 18-hole Jack Nicklaus Signature golf course. Two boat ramps are available in the park along with rentals. Hiking trails from .25-5 miles are located throughout the park.

Sideling Hill

Hancock MD
www.mgs.md.gov/geology/geology_tour/sideling_hill.html

One of the best rock exposures in Maryland and indeed in the entire northeastern United States is located approximately 6 miles west of Hancock in Washington County, where Interstate 68 cuts through Sideling Hill. Almost 810 feet of strata in a tightly folded syncline are exposed in this road cut. Although other exposures may surpass Sideling Hill in either thickness of exposed strata or in quality of geologic structure, few can equal its combination of both. This exposure is an excellent outdoor classroom where students of geology can observe and examine various sedimentary rock types, structural features, and geomorphic relationships. The Maryland State Highways Administration permanently closed the Sideling Hill Visitor Center located on the eastern side of the hill; however, the parking lot, paved walkways, observation bridge and restrooms remain open.

Six Flags America and Paradise Island Water Park

13710 Central Avenue
Mitchellville MD 20721
www.sixflags.com/america
301.249.1331

The park features eight roller coasters including the steel theme coasters, "Batwing" and "Superman Ride of Steel," as well as a water park. "Looney Toons Movie Town" features 12 rides and attractions for younger children and parents.

South Mountain Creamery

8305 Bolivar Road
Middletown MD 21769
www.southmountaincreamery.com/home.php
301.371.8565

Feed calves, watch cows being milked, or see the farm at this family-owned dairy and milk-processing plant. South Mountain Creamery boasts that it is Maryland's only on-the-farm processing plant, where they grow the crops, milk the cows, process the milk and deliver the goods.

South Mountain Recreation Area

21843 National Pike
Boonsboro MD 21712
www.dnr.state.md.us/publiclands/western/southmountain.asp
301.791.4767

This recreation area encompasses four state parks. Greenbrier State Park is a multi-use park with picnic sites, swimming, boating, hiking, fishing, and camping available. Washington Monument State Park features the first monument built in honor of George Washington (1827). Other features include hiking, day-use area, picnic sites, and pavilions for rent. Guthland State Park was the site of the Battle of South Mountain (September, 14, 1862) as part of Lee's Maryland campaign. This site was also the estate of George Alfred Townsend, writer and civil war correspondent, and includes the War Correspondents Memorial. South Mountain State Park runs the length of South Mountain on the border between Washington and Frederick Counties. It is mostly wooded and features the 38-mile section of the Appalachian Trail.

Walkersville Southern Railroad

34 W Pennsylvania Avenue
Walkersville MD 21793
www.wsrr.org
301.898.0899

The Walkersville Southern Railroad runs on the Frederick
Branch of the old Pennsylvania Railroad. The turn-of-the-
century railroad station, ticket office and freight house add to
the feel of a trip back in time. Passengers ride a vintage 1920s
car, caboose or an open flat car into picturesque Maryland farm
country at speeds limited to 10 mph.

Western Maryland Scenic Railroad

13 Chesapeake & Ohio Canal National Historic Park
Cumberland MD 21502
www.wmsr.com
301.759.4400

From Cumberland, take a three-and-a-half hour trip through the
Allegheny Mountains on Mountain Thunder. The 1916 Baldwin
steam engine chugs through rugged countryside, climbing
1,300 feet over 16 miles of track through a 900-foot tunnel
and around horseshoe curves. The train stops for a layover in
Frostburg, where you can have lunch at the Old Depot and visit
the Thrasher Carriage Museum.

VIRGINIA

Busch Gardens Williamsburg

1 Busch Gardens Boulevard
Williamsburg VA 22185
www.buschgardens.com
800.343.7946

Apollo's Chariot roller coaster and the Escape from Pompeii
boat ride are among the attractions at Busch Gardens
Williamsburg. Animal attractions at Busch Garden include
Budweiser Clydesdales and an eagle habitat.

Dinosaur Land

3848 Stonewall Jackson Highway
White Post VA 22663
www.dinosaurland.com
540.869.2222

After a visit to Skyline Caverns (see page 187), be sure to plan a quick stop at Dinosaur Land. Children will love to romp among the 36 life-size fiberglass dinosaurs, prehistoric mammals and fanciful creatures in a shaded outside setting. Take a self-guided tour of the dinosaurs; there are explanatory signs beside each one. This is a great place for taking photos!

Flying Circus Air Show

5114 Ritchie Road
Bealeton VA
www.flyingcircusairshow.com
540.439.8661

The Flying Circus Air Show in Bealeton has 200 acres of Antique Airfields and performs every Sunday at 2:30 pm from May through October. From parachute jumpers to wing walkers, audiences are thrilled and amazed. Gates open up at 11 am.

Lake Anna State Park

6800 Lawyers Road
Spotsylvania VA 22551
www.dcr.virginia.gov/state_parks/lak.shtml
540.854.5503

For families looking for a fun day-trip to a lake, an outing to Lake Anna State Park, located just south of Fredericksburg, is just the answer. Only 90 minutes from DC, Lake Anna offers a fresh water lake for swimming, boating, fishing, and water-skiing. The state park features a sandy, life-guarded beach, wooded hiking trails, playground, and concession stand, as well as a stocked kids-only fishing pond. Nearby marinas rent boats and jet skis by the day or half day. Bring a picnic and have a great day!

Leesburg Animal Park

19270 Monroe-Madison Memorial Highway
Leesburg VA 20175
www.leesburganimalpark.com
703.433.0002

This petting zoo is home to farm animals such as cows, chickens, and goats, as well as to more exotic animals such as llamas, a zebra, and a tiger. Visitors can purchase food to feed the animals, enjoy a pony or elephant ride, and observe wild animals up close.

Luray Caverns

101 Cave Hill Road
Luray VA 22835
www.luraycaverns.com
540.743.6551

Tour the largest and most popular cavern in eastern America. The profusion of formations and the variety of natural colors make this an underground wonderland. Hear the Great Stalagpipe Organ. See monumental columns, rooms with ceilings more than ten stories high, shimmering draperies, crystal clear pools, and glittering, glistening stone. Children will be amazed by the colorful formations. Admission also includes The Historic Car and Carriage Caravan Museum. Tours last just over an hour.

Monticello: The Home of Thomas Jefferson

931 Thomas Jefferson Parkway
Charlottesville VA 22902
www.monticello.org
434.984.9800

Get up close at the house Thomas Jefferson built for himself and his family in the Piedmont region of Central Virginia. The guided house tour covers the rooms in Monticello and lasts about 30 minutes. Admission includes access to the grounds and two optional outdoor guided tours, in season: the Plantation Community and the Gardens and Grounds.

National Museum of the Marine Corps

18900 Jefferson Davis Highway
Triangle VA 22134
www.usmcmuseum.org
877.635.1775

The National Museum of the Marine Corps is located on
a 135-acre site just off I-95 next to the Marine Corps Base
at Quantico, VA, 30 miles south of Washington, DC. The
architecture is inspired by the Flag Raising at Iwo Jima, with
a 210-foot tilted mast and glass atrium and a 160-foot atrium
housing the central gallery. Galleries hold permanent and changing
exhibits on Marine Corps history, an interactive Boot Camp
exhibit, and other exhibits about the Marine Corps experience.

New Market Battlefield Military Museum

8895 George R Collins Parkway
New Market VA 22844
www2.vmi.edu/museum/nm
866.515.1864

Atop this small hill is the actual New Market Battlefield and
museum. The museum is a rendition of General Lee's famed
Arlington House. The focus is primarily Civil War, however
the collection of military memorabilia, relics, uniforms, flags,
weapons, etc. from the American Revolution to the present is
one of the largest on display. Fourteen marble and granite troop
position markers dot the landscape and forever mark the Union
and Confederate soldiers who fought and died here. There are
walking paths and a wooded picnic area.

Paramount's Kings Dominion

16000 Theme Park Way
Doswell VA 23047
www.kingsdominion.com
804.876.5000

Kings Dominion is a 400-acre theme park including Water
Works Water Park. Kidzville and Nickeloden on Central provide
rides and activities for preschoolers through elementary age.
Concerts and special events are scheduled throughout the
season. Older children and teens will find a dozen coasters and
thrill rides.

Pink Box Visitors Center, Middleburg

12 North Madison Street
Middleburg VA 20117
www.visitmiddleburgva.com
540.687.5888

Middleburg is an historic, rural village in the heart of Virginia Hunt Country. Antique shops, specialty stores, and great restaurants abound. Three top wineries and the Glenwood Park Race Course are just minutes away.

Shenandoah National Park

Stanley VA 22851
www.nps.gov/shen
540.999.3500

The Shenandoah National Park contains over 196,000 acres and lies across the crest of the Blue Ridge Mountains in Virginia. Skyline Drive, a winding road that runs through the park, provides vistas of the spectacular landscape. This land was previously used by mountain farmers for grazing sheep and cattle, farming, and hunting. The park was established in 1935 to bring the National Park experience to the millions of people living "within a day's drive," along the east coast. Trails totaling more than 500 miles provide short or long hiking adventures. Visitors can see plants and animals and experience the beauty and peace of this vast national park. Shenandoah is a wonderful place to experience fall foliage!

Skyline Caverns

10334 Stonewall Jackson Highway
Front Royal VA 22630
www.skylinecaverns.com
540.625.4545

When making a trip to Shenandoah National Park, don't miss the opportunity to visit the beautiful and unusual Skyline Caverns. These underground caves are filled with amazing geological formations that inspire the imagination while offering real life lessons about the physical history of the earth. The 60 million year old caverns remained a secret until 1937 when they were first discovered.

Bring along a sweater, as the temperature inside is 54 degrees all year round. The best way to see the caverns is on a guided walking tour conducted by a member of the knowledgeable staff. It lasts about an hour and covers just over one mile. The spectacular lighting brings to life the aptly named wonders beneath the earth: the Capitol Dome, the Rainbow Trail, the Wishing Well, the Shrine, and Fairyland Lake to name a few. There are also three underground streams, one of which forms a lovely 37-foot waterfall. Amidst all this magic, the constant dripping of water throughout the caverns teaches children how the formations are made, and just how long it takes nature to do the work. Anchorites, call "orchids of the mineral kingdom," grow an inch every seven thousand years. After the tour, enjoy a half-mile ride on the miniature train and have a picnic on the wooded grounds. Also be sure to visit nearby Dinosaur Land, see page 184.

HARPERS FERRY, WEST VIRGINIA

Harpers Ferry National Historical Park

171 Shoreline Drive
Harpers Ferry WV 25425
www.nps.gov/hafe
304.535.6029

As you begin your tour of Harpers Ferry, look for the Information Center where you will get an overview of the six main park themes: local industry, John Brown's raid, the Civil War, African-American history, transportation, and environment. In addition to the museums listed below, there are hiking trails accessible from the town and fishing in the river nearby (licenses are required).

Black History Museum: This museum is devoted to the history of slaves and their struggle to gain freedom. It includes information before the Civil War and afterwards.

Storer College Museum: Learn the history of the college that educated freedmen after the Civil War.

John Brown's Fort: This was the armory's fire-engine house, used by John Brown as a refuge during his 1859 raid. Located at the corner of Shenandoah and Potomac Streets.

John Brown Museum: On Shenandoah Street, look for this museum relating the events of John Brown's raid. Video presentations describe the events leading to the raid and its immediate effects on the country.

Civil War Museum: Located on High Street, the museum depicts the way that the Civil War affected the town of Harpers Ferry. During the war, the town was occupied by either the Union or Confederate Armies.

Harper House: Built in 1782, this is the oldest surviving structure in the park. Climb the stone steps leading uphill from High Street to reach this historic site.

Dry Goods Store, Provost Marshall's Office, Blacksmith Shop: On Shenandoah Street, there are good places to visit to appreciate the social and economic history of the times. In the summer, the office and shops are staffed with people in period clothing.

PENNSYLVANIA

Bedford Park and Museum

110 Fort Bedford Drive
Bedford PA 15522
www.fortbedfordmuseum.org
814.623.8891

Tour this re-creation of a French 1758 stockade fort from the French and Indian War. Artifacts from the war are on display here. They include flintlock rifles, early clothing, and antique hand tools. Discover the history of Fort Bedford and the pioneer days on the frontier of western Pennsylvania.

Dutch Wonderland

2249 Lincoln Highway
Lancaster PA 17602
www.dutchwonderland.com
866.386.2839

Knights, dragons and princesses are the backdrop for Dutch Wonderland Amusement Park. Geared for children 12 and younger, Dutch Wonderland includes rides, water play and miniature golf.

Eisenhower National Historic Site

1195 Baltimore Pike
Gettysburg PA 17325
www.nps.gov/eise
717.338.9114

During the Eisenhower presidency from 1955 to 1961, the farm now known as the Eisenhower National Historic Site served as the president's weekend retreat, a refuge in times of illness, and a relaxed setting in which to meet with world leaders like Premier Khruschev and President Charles de Gaulle. It was a working farm as well with fertile cropland and a show herd of black Angus cattle. The Eisenhowers deeded the farm to the National Park Service in 1967. A visit to the farm includes a tour of the Eisenhower home, which retains all its original furnishings. Self-guided walks throughout the site's 690 acres allow for exploration of the skeet range, putting green, rose gardens, guest house, black Angus herd, and barns still housing Eisenhower vehicles and farm equipment. In season, living history and park ranger programs are offered. A reception center features a video and exhibits on Eisenhower's life, including his military career.

Explore & More

20 East High Street
Gettysburg PA 17325
www.exploreandmore.com
717.337.9151

This hands-on children's museum and playhouse is designed for ages 4 to 8 and includes a Civil War playhouse with general store and battlefield encampment, a construction zone, giant bubbles, and an art room.

Gettysburg National Military Park

Gettysburg PA
www.nps.gov/gett/index.htm
717.334.1124

This park is the site of a major battle of the American Civil War. The three days of fighting on July 1, 2, and 3, 1863, are considered a turning point in the war and marked the second and final invasion of the North by Confederate forces. The Gettysburg National Cemetery adjoins the park and is where

Abraham Lincoln delivered his famous Gettysburg Address.
The Visitor Center is located south of the town of Gettysburg
and is accessible from Routes 15 and 134. If you begin here,
you will get tour information, see the Rosensteel Collection of
Civil War artifacts, and see an electronic map of the battle. The
first show starts at 8:15 am and is held every 45 minutes until
closing. The Cyclorama Center, adjacent to the Visitor Center,
contains the Famous Cyclorama painting of "Pickett's Charge"
by Paul Philippoteaux in 1884. The painting is displayed with
a dramatic sound and light program. There are no advance
reservations. Groups are admitted in order of arrival. This
center also contains a number of free exhibits.

Ghosts of Gettysburg Candlelight Walking Tours

271 Baltimore Street
Gettysburg PA 17325
www.ghostsofgettysburg.com
717.337.0445

These tours are popular evening destinations. They are based
on the *Ghosts of Gettysburg* trilogy by Mark Nesbitt. Trained
guides in 19th century garb take stories from Nesbitt's best-
selling books and turn them into a fascinating hour and fifteen-
minute stroll through the darkened streets of Gettysburg. Each
tour covers about a mile of leisurely walking and contains about
ten different "haunted" sites.

Hershey Gardens

170 Hotel Road
Hershey PA 17033
www.hersheygardens.org
717.534.3492

This 23-acre botanical garden, home to spectacular annuals and
perennials, rare specimen trees and much more, was founded
by Milton Hershey in 1937. Its award-winning rose garden
has over 7000 roses and is one of the largest of its kind in the
United States. Hershey Gardens has one of the largest outdoor
butterfly houses in Pennsylvania, featuring 300 North American
butterflies. The Children's Garden offers interactive learning
experiences and fun with gardens and plants.

Hershey Park

100 W Hersheypark Drive
Hershey PA 17033
www.hersheypark.com
717.534.3860

Hershey Park is a world-class theme park with more than
60 rides and attractions and more than six hours of live
entertainment daily. "Roller Soaker" is the first interactive water
coaster in the Northeast. Hershey Park is home to nine thrilling
roller coasters and seven drenching water rides. In addition,
there are more than 20 rides designed especially for younger
guests. Admission to Zoo America North American Wildlife
Park is also included in a one-price admission to Hershey Park.
Enjoy Hershey's Chocolate World visitors center, the official
visitors center of Hershey Foods Corporation. Travel like a coca
bean from a typical jungle though the factory manufacturing
process and learn how chocolate is made and receive a free
sample at the end of the tour. Also fun is "Hershey's Really BIG
3-D Show"—a three-dimensional musical adventure featuring
the famous Hershey's product characters. While you're there,
take a tour of the town on the Hershey Trolley or learn about
the man behind the chocolate—Milton S. Hershey at the
Hershey Museum, which features a Discovery Room especially
for children.

Knoebels Amusement Park and Resort

391 Knoebels Boulevard
Elysburg PA 17824
www.knoebels.com
570.672.2572

This no-admission, pay-per-ride amusement park (most rides
are $1 or less) boasts excellent roller coasters, swimming,
water slides and campgrounds—and a park well-suited to the
youngest visitors. Knoebels has a less commercial feel than other
amusement parks; a family of four can buy $40 worth of tickets
for the day.

The Land of Little Horses

125 Glenwood Drive
Gettysburg PA 17325
www.landoflittlehorses.com
717.334.7259

Enjoy this animal park featuring performing Falabella miniature horses and a petting farm with many other animals. The little horses, originally bred in Argentina, stand as small as 26" high. Also see shows, a nature trail, barn displays, and much more.

Old Bedford Village

220 Sawblade Road
Bedford PA 15522
www.oldbedfordvillage.com
814.623.1156

The butcher, the baker, the candlestick maker...children will find them all, practicing their crafts at Old Bedford Village in Bedford, Pennsylvania. Parents and kids alike will enjoy stepping back in time as they tour this pioneer-era village (1750-1850) featuring over 40 reproduction and authentic log, stone, and frame structures. There are two schools, a church, a general store, and plenty of pioneers in period clothing cooking and farming. You can also see crafts people demonstrating the rigor of every day living or one of over 14 period crafts. About a two-hour drive from the Washington metropolitan area, Old Bedford Village merits an all-day trip. In addition to the historical village, families can enjoy hiking, camping, fishing, and picnicking.

Strasburg Railroad

301 Gap Road
Ronks PA 17572
www.strasburgrailroad.com
717.687.7522

Explore the rail engines and rail cars close up on America's oldest short-line railroad. See restored trains, including a full-size, coal-burning steam train and ride in coaches or in the open air for a 45-minute ride through the country side. Certain rides stop for a picnic lunch. Ride the miniature Cagney Steam Train. Operate a hand-powered Pump Car or watch little ones steer the pint-size Cranky Car. Tour the switch tower and freight equipment displays. Arrive at least 45 to 60 minutes early, particularly on special event days. Weekends are crowded. Wear comfortable, closed-toed shoes for walking on rocks, gravel and sand. Beware of sitting close to the engine on the steam train with little ones in tow as ashes and soot can fall on passengers sitting close to the coal car.

ZooAmerica, North American Wildlife Park

201 Park Avenue
Hershey PA 17033
www.zooamerica.com
717.534.3900

This 11-acre walk-through zoo features over 200 animals representing five regions of North America. Can be included in a one-price admission to Hershey Park.

Field Trips

Going Places with Children in Washington, DC originated half a century ago as a photocopied list of the many field trips students take as part of Green Acres School's hands-on, experiential curriculum. For this new edition, the editors asked current teachers about their favorite field trips—trips that families or groups could take both for education and for fun. This wide-ranging sample is meant to serve as a jumping-off point for ideas for families and teachers looking for ways to bring to life topics their children are studying in school, from math to art to social studies. Please note that many other entries in the book would be available for field trips, we have simply highlighted a few that Green Acres students participate in.

PRE-KINDERGARTEN

Bethesda Chevy Chase Rescue Squad

5020 Battery Lane
Bethesda MD 20814
www.bcrrs.org
301.652.0077

This trip is taken during the unit on transportation. The children experience the sights, sounds, and learn the importance of emergency teams and vehicles. They are given the opportunity to sit in a fire truck, ambulance, or whatever vehicles are available at the time of the visit. The tour is guided by an experienced EMT.

Congressional Aquarium

138 Congressional Lane
Rockville MD 20852
www.congressionalaquarium.com
301.881.6182

The children are exposed to a large variety of fish in small aquariums, guided by a knowledgeable employee with expertise in fresh and salt water fish and aquatic plants. Questions are welcomed and plenty of time is given for children to peruse the tanks. Sometimes the tour guide has taken out a fish for closer inspection. It is a culminating activity for the sea life unit of study.

Great Harvest Bread Company

12668 Rockville Pike
Rockville MD 20852
www.greatharvestrockville.com
301.770.8544

At the end of the unit on families, traditions, and food, we take this trip to mark the closure of the unit. The children experience the entire process of baking bread, from the grinding of the wheat to the baking of the loaf. They each sample a slice of bread at the end of the tour, and leave with a small loaf to take home.

KINDERGARTEN

Adventure Playground

17920 Germantown Park Drive
Germantown MD 20841
www.montgomeryparks.org/facilities/south_germantown

The children are provided with the opportunity to explore, climb, run, slide, swing, and jump on a vast array of equipment that is new and different to them, followed by a picnic lunch on site. Restroom and a water fountain are available close to the playground area. This is a fun end of the year celebratory outing!

Adventure Theatre

7300 MacArthur Blvd
Glen Echo MD 20812
www.adventuretheatre-mtc.org
301.634.2270

The children are introduced to live theater in a small, cozy
environment with stories that are familiar and age appropriate.
It is a wonderful way to expose children to the performing arts.

Black Hill Regional Park

20926 Lake Ridge Drive,
Boyds MD 20841
www.montgomeryparks.org/facilities/regional_parks/blackhill
301.528.3490

This is an outdoor educational experience observing nature
and the changing of seasons. In addition, this is a community
building activity, as we go early in the school year and invite all
families to join us.

College Park Aviation Museum

1985 Corporal Frank Scott Drive
College Park MD 20740
www.collegeparkaviationmuseum.com
301.864.6029

The children are expertly guided through a history of aviation
via a collection of unique aircraft and artifacts. They have the
opportunity to sit in and "fly" a plane, and then make a paper
airplane of their own to launch. It is a culminating activity for
the transportation unit of study.

Imagination Stage

4908 Auburn Avenue
Bethesda MD 20814
www.imaginiationstage.org
301.961.6060

This trip provides exposure to live theater performance.
Programs are chosen related to our themes of study.

Smithsonian Discovery Theater

The Ripley Center
1100 Jefferson Drive SW
Washington DC 20560
www.discoverytheater.org
202.633.8700

This trip provides exposure to live theater performance. Programs are chosen related to our themes of study.

FIRST & SECOND GRADE

Audubon Naturalist Society

8940 Jones Mill Road
Chevy Chase MD 20815
www.audubonnaturalist.org
301.652.9188

This trip provides the opportunity to explore nature and observe animal habitats and the change of seasons.

Brookside Gardens "Wings of Fancy"

1500 Glenallan Avenue
Wheaton MD 20902
www.montgomeryparks.org/brookside/wings_of_fancy
301.962.1453

Why did the caterpillar hatch on the milkweed? To get a yummy dinner. Learn about these wonderful creatures, and be surrounded by butterflies from all over the world flying freely inside the Conservatory. The first and second graders study the life cycle of the monarch butterfly and its migration pattern.

Homestead Farm

15604 Sugarland Road
Poolesville MD 20837
www.homestead-farm.net
301.977.3761

It is wonderful to see the leaves changing colors and appreciate the beauty fall has to offer. First and second graders traditionally every year go to Homestead Farm to observe the signs of fall, enjoy a hay ride and pick pumpkins. They also have an opportunity to visit with the animals on the farm.

This trip is a fall tradition the Primary Unit students experience together as a community to observe the signs of fall and enjoy each other's company.

Kennedy Center Family Theater

2700 F Street NW
Washington DC 20566
www.kennedy-center.org
202.467.4600

This trip provides exposure to live theater performance. Programs are chosen related to our themes of study.

National Zoo

3001 Connecticut Avenue NW
Washington DC 20008
www.nationalzoo.si.edu
202.633.4888

This field trip is an extension of our reptile unit of study.

THIRD GRADE

Claude Moore Farm at Turkey Run

6310 Georgetown Pike
McLean VA 22101
www.1771.org
703.442.7557

Tour a traditionally re-created colonial farm with 'actors' presenting as Colonial farm hands and families. See the tobacco house and a small home. There is an interactive section with authentic activities including dipping candles, carding wool, grinding maize, and playing traditional colonial games.

C&O Canal Barge Ride at Great Falls

11710 MacArthur Boulevard
Potomac MD 20854
www.nps.gov/choh/index.htm
301.739.4200

This trip is a guided tour through Great Falls on a mule-pulled boat ride through the locks and up a portion of the canal with a narration of early canal life.

Historic St. Mary's City

18751 Hogaboom Lane
St. Marys City MD 20686
www.stmaryscity.org
240.895.4990

Visit a Woodland Indian Hamlet, the Maryland Dove, the Town Center which includes colonial hotels and printing, and the Godiah Spray Tobacco Plantation. Our third graders enjoy the guided tours and activities to learn about early Colonial Life.

The Lyceum, Alexandria's History Museum

201 S. Washington Street
Alexandria VA 22314
www.alexandriava.gov
703.746.4994

This guided tour of Old Town Alexandria provides a visual connection to the third grade studies of Colonial times.

Sandy Spring Museum

17901 Bentley Road
Sandy Spring MD 20860
www.sandyspringmuseum.org
301.774.0022

This is a hands-on learning experience with a blacksmith in an authentic setting. This fantastic trip complements the third grade studies of early Maryland history during the Colonial time period.

Thunderbird American Indian Dancers

Goucher College
1021 Delaney Road
Towson MD 21204
www.ArtsonStage.org
410.252.8717

The students watch authentic Native American dancing from various tribes across the United States. Regalia is discussed by region. The trip correlates with the third grade studies of Native Americans.

FOURTH GRADE

Hard Bargain Farm Environmental Center

2001 Bryan Point Road
Accokeek MD 20607
www.fergusonfoundation.org/hard-bargain-farm
301.292.5665

This environmental study center has regular days open for the public. Farming practices as well as environmental preservation of the Potomac River are studied. The fourth grade overnight includes both those elements, introducing children to milking cows, collecting eggs and other practices of where food comes from. In addition to the outdoor curriculum, this field trip is about teamwork and community building. Shared chores and responsibilities, as well as regular journaling and reflection make this an important experience for individuals as well as the group as a whole.

National Aquarium in Baltimore

501 E Pratt Street
Baltimore MD 21202
www.aqua.org
410.576.3833 (Group Reservations)

The aquarium displays many wildlife environments across the globe. The rainforest exhibit contains plants and animals from the Amazon. This trip jumpstarts the fourth grade's study of the rainforest and the detailed research they will conduct on plants and animals.

National Building Museum

401 F Street NW
Washington DC 20001
www.nbm.org
202.272.2448

The building itself is a study of geometric shapes and architectural significance. The program the fourth grade attends is "Fuller's Fantastic Geodesic Dome." It connects to 2- and 3-D geometry in math class studies.

U.S. Botanic Garden Conservatory

100 Maryland Avenue SE
Washington DC 20001
www.usbg.gov
202.225.8333

Using the various rooms in the conservatory, the children go on
a scavenger hunt to different natural environments. Geography,
Explorers and Creative Writing are touchstones for this trip.
Specimens from across the world are included. Examples of
spices and plants brought over during the age of exploration
are "discovered." In addition the sights, sounds and smells are
fodder for beautiful writing.

FIFTH & SIXTH GRADE

Maryland Science Center

601 Light Street
Baltimore MD 21230
www.mdsci.org
410.685.2370

The museum has several exhibit halls that contain hands-
on activities for students. These halls are free to Maryland
students. Chaperone requirements are 1 adult to 10 students.
For a reasonable fee there is also access to an IMAX theater,
planetarium and hands-on workshops. Sixth graders visited the
Mummies exhibit (temporary) to support the science and social
studies "Civilization" unit. Human Body exhibits to support the
sixth grade science curriculum.

Phillip Merrill Environmental Center—Chesapeake Bay Foundation

6 Herndon Avenue
Annapolis MD 21403
www.cbf.org/join-us/education-program/apply-for-an-education-program
410.268.8816

Fifth graders attend this exciting trip sponsored by the
Chesapeake Bay Foundation. To complement their studies of
the state of Maryland, fifth graders continue to learn about
water quality and crabbing as they take an adventure on the
Chesapeake Bay. They also have the opportunity to canoe and
examine water quality and runoff in a local waterway.

Index

A

Adventure Park at Sandy Spring Friends School, The, 79

Adventure Playground, 196

Adventure Theatre, 111, 197

AFI Silver Theatre and Cultural Center. See American Film Institute; AFI Silver Theatre and Cultural Center

African-American Civil War Memorial and Museum, The, 20

African American History and Culture. See Anacostia Museum and Center for African American History and Culture

African Art. See National Museum of African Art

African Art Museum of Maryland, 37

Air and Space Center. See Steven F. Udvar-Hazy Air and Space Center

Air and Space Museum. See National Air and Space Museum

Airpark. See Montgomery County Airpark

Alexandria Archaeology Museum, 49

Alexandria Black History Resource Center, 49

Alexandria City Hall. See Market Square/Alexandria City Hall

Alexandria Convention and Visitor's Bureau, 1

Alexandria's History Museum. See Lyceum, Alexandria's History Museum, The

Algonkian Regional Park, 79
Downpour, 146

A Likely Story Children's Bookstore, 129

Allen Pond Park, 80

All Fired Up, 157

American Film Institute; AFI Silver Theatre and Cultural Center, 112

American History. See National Museum of American History

American Indian Museum. See National Museum of the American Indian

American University Museum. See Katzen Arts Center/American University Museum

American Visionary Art Museum, 167

Anacostia Museum and Center for African American History and Culture, 20

Anacostia Park, 59

Annapolis Conference Center and Visitor's Bureau, 1

Antietam National Battlefield, 72

Apothecary Shop and Museum. See Stabler-Leadbeater Apothecary Shop and Museum

Aquarium. See National Aquarium in Baltimore

Arena Stage, 112

Arlington Cinema 'n' Drafthouse, 112

Arlington House/The Robert E. Lee Memorial, 50

Arlington National Cemetery, 50

Arlington Public Schools Planetarium, 90

Artisan Confections, 161

Asian Art Museum. See Freer Sackler/The Smithsonian's Museum of Asian Art

A Tour de Force, 3

Audrey Moore/Wakefield Park and Recreation Center, 80

Audubon Naturalist Sanctuary Shop, 129

Audubon Naturalist Society, 198. See Rust Sanctuary; See Webb Sanctuary; See Woodend Nature Sanctuary

Autobahn Indoor Speedway, The, 154

Aviation Museum. See College Park Aviation Museum

B

Babe Ruth Museum, 167

Ball's Bluff Regional Park, 72

Baltimore and Ohio Railroad Museum, 168

Baltimore Civil War Museum, The/President Street Station, 168

Baltimore Maritime Museum, 168

Baltimore Museum of Art, 169

Baltimore Museum of Industry, 169

Baltimore Orioles, 101

Baltimore Ravens, 101

Baltimore Streetcar Museum, 169

Baltimore Visitor Center, 2

Baltimore Zoo, The, 170

Banneker-Douglass Museum, 163

Barnes and Noble, 129

Barston's Child's Play, 130

Basilica of the National Shrine of the Immaculate Conception, 21

Battery-Kemble Park, 59

Baysox. *See* Bowie Baysox

Beall-Dawson House and Stonestreet Museum of 19th Century Medicine, 37

Bedford Park and Museum, 189

Belair Mansion, 38

Belair Stable, 38

Belle Haven Marina, 106

Bethesda Chevy Chase Rescue Squad, 195

Black Hill Regional Park, 61, 197

Black History. *See* Alexandria Black History Resource Center

Black History Museum. *See* Harpers Ferry National Historical Park

Blackrock Center for the Arts, 113

Bluemont Park, 81

Blue Planet SCUBA, 145

B'nai B'rith Klutznick National Jewish Museum, 21

Bohrer Water Park at Summit Hall Farm, 145

Botanic Garden. *See* U.S. Botanic Garden

Bowie Baysox, 102

Bowie Skate Park, 135

Bowie Train Station and Huntington Museum, 38

Bowl America Gaithersburg, 153

Bowlmor Lanes, 153

Boyds Historical Society, 38

Brambleton Regional Park, 81, 109

Breezy Point Beach, 177

Brookside Gardens, 76

Brookside Gardens "Wings of Fancy", 198

Brookside Nature Center, 90

Bull Run Marina, 67

Bull Run Regional Park, 81

Bureau of Engraving and Printing, 21

Burke Lake Park, 82

Busch Gardens Williamsburg, 183

Butler's Orchard, 74

C

Cabin John Ice Rink, 135

Cabin John Regional Park, 82

Cal Ripken Collegiate Baseball League, 102

Calvert Cliffs State Park, 61

Calvert Marine Museum, 177

Cameron Run Regional Park and Great Waves Water Park, 82

Candy Cane City, 83

Capital Crescent Trail, 60

Capitals. *See* Washington Capitals

Capitol Hill, 18

   Capitol, The, 18

   Eastern Market, 18

   Folger Shakespeare Library, 18

   Library of Congress, 19

   National Postal Museum, 19

   U.S. Supreme Court, 20

Capitol, The, 18

Carlyle House Historic Park, 50

Carroll County Farm Museum, 97

Castle, The. *See* Smithsonian Institution Information Center

Catoctin Mountain Park, 62

Catoctin Wildlife Preserve and Zoo, 177

Cedar Hill. *See* Frederick Douglass Home

Cedarville State Forest, 62

Center for African American History and Culture. *See* Anacostia Museum and Center for African American History and Culture

Cherry Blossom Festival, 125

Chesapeake and Ohio (C&O) Canal, 62

Chesapeake Beach Railway Museum, 178

Chesapeake Beach Water Park, 178

Chesapeake Children's Museum, The, 164

Children's Museum of Rose Hill Manor Park, The, 179

Child's Play. *See* Barston's Child's Play

Chinquapin Park Recreation Center & Aquatics Facility, 83

Chocolate Chocolate, 162

Chocolate Factory. *See* SPAGnVOLA Chocolate Factory Tour

Christ Church, 51

Cinema 'n' Drafthouse. *See* Arlington Cinema 'n' Drafthouse

Civil War Medicine. *See* National Museum of Civil War Medicine

Civil War Museum. *See* Harpers Ferry National Historical Park

Clara Barton National Historic Site, 39

Claude Moore Colonial Farm at Turkey Run, 98

Claude Moore Farm at Turkey Run, 199

Claude Moore Recreation Center, 146

Clay Café Studio, 158

Clearwater Nature Center, 91

Clemyjontri Park, 84

C&O Canal. *See* Chesapeake and Ohio (C&O) Canal

C&O Canal Barge Ride at Great Falls, 199

College Park Aviation Museum, 39, 197

Color Me Mine, 158

Colvin Run Mill Historic Site, 51

Comedy Sportz. *See* The Comedy Spot/Comedy Sportz

Congressional Aquarium, 195

Constitution Gardens, 8

Convention and Visitors Association, Washington, DC, 3

Corcoran Gallery of Art, 22

Cosca Regional Park, 63

Cox Farms, 74

Crime and Punishment Museum, 22

Croydon Creek Nature Center, 91

Cryptologic Museum and National Vigilance Park. *See* National Cryptologic Museum and National Vigilance Park

Cunningham Falls State Park, 63

D

DASH, 5

Daughters of the American Revolution Museum, 22

DC United, 103

Deep Creek Lake State Park, 179

Dentistry Museum. *See* National Museum of Dentistry

Dickerson Conservation Area, 63

Dick's Sporting Goods, 156

Dinosaur Land, 184

Dolcezza Artisanal Gelato, 161

Drug Enforcement Administration Museum and Visitors Center, 51

Duck Tours, DC, 4

Dumbarton Oaks Gardens and Museum, 23

Dutch Wonderland, 189

Dynamite Gym, 154

E

Earth Treks Climbing Center, 157

Eastern Market, 18

East Potomac Park, 84

Eisenhower National Historic Site, 190

Ellipse Visitor's Pavilion, 2

Encore Stage and Studio, 113

Engraving and Printing. *See* Bureau of Engraving and Printing

Explore & More, 190

Explorers Hall, National Geographic Society, 23

F

Fairfax Ice Arena, 136

Fairfax Symphony Orchestra, 114

Fairland Recreational Park/Fairland Regional Park, 84

Fairy Godmother, 130

FDR Memorial. *See* Roosevelt, Franklin Delano, Memorial

Federal Hill Park, 170

Fire Museum, 170

Flag Ponds Nature Park, 179

Fletcher's Boathouse, 106

Flying Circus Air Show, 184

Folger Shakespeare Library, 18

Folger Shakespeare Theatre, 114

Ford's Theatre, Lincoln Museum, Petersen House, 23

Fort Dupont Ice Arena, 136

Fort McHenry National Monument and Historic Shrine, 171

Fort Ward Museum and Historic Site, 52

Fort Ward Park, 73

Fort Washington Park, 73

Fountainhead Regional Park, 68

Franciscan Monastery, 24

Frederick Douglass Home (Cedar Hill), 24

Frederick Keys, 103

Fredericksburg and Spotsylvania National Military Park, 73

Freer Sackler/The Smithsonian's Museum of Asian Art, 8

Friendship Firehouse, 52

Friendship Park. See Turtle Park; See Turtle Park (aka Friendship Park)

Frying Pan Park, Kidwell Farm, 98

Funfit's Organically Grown Gym, 154

G

Gadsby's Tavern Museum, 52

Gaithersburg Skate Park, 136

Gardens Ice House, 137

Georgetown Cupcake, 159

George Washington Masonic National Memorial, 53

Germantown Indoor Swim Center, 147

Germantown Recreational Park. See South Germantown Recreational Park

Gettysburg National Military Park, 190

Ghosts of Gettysburg Candlelight Walking Tours, 191

Glen Echo Park and Carousel, 40
    Adventure Theatre, 111
    Puppet Company Playhouse, 121

Glover-Archbold Park, 60

Goddard Space Flight Center. See NASA/Goddard Space Flight Center

Good Knight Kingdom Museum, 40

Great Falls Park, 68

Great Harvest Bread Company, 196

Great Waves Water Park. See Cameron Run Regional Park and Great Waves Water Park

Greenbelt Museum, 41

Greenbelt Park, 64

Greenbrier State Park, 180

Green Spring Gardens Park, 77

Gulf Branch Nature Center, 91

Gunston Hall Plantation, 53

H

Hadley's Park, 85

Hagerstown Speedway, 103

Harborplace and The Gallery, 171

Hard Bargain Farm Environmental Center, 201

Harper House. See Harpers Ferry National Historical Park

Harpers Ferry National Historical Park, 188
    Black History Museum, 188
    Blacksmith Shop, 189
    Civil War Museum, 189
    Dry Goods Store, 189
    Harper House, 189
    John Brown Museum, 189
    John Brown's Fort, 188
    Provost Marshall's Office, 189
    Storer College Museum, 188

Hello Cupcake, 160

Hemlock Overlook Regional Park, 85

Henson's, Josiah, Cabin. See Uncle Tom's Cabin

Herbert W. Wells Ice Rink, 137

Hershey Gardens, 191

Hershey Park, 192

Hidden Oaks Nature Center, 92

Hidden Pond Nature Center, 92

Hill's Gymnastic Training Center, 155

Hillwood Museum and Garden, 24

Hirshhorn Museum and Sculpture Garden, 9

Historical Society of Washington, DC, 25

Historic Annapolis Foundation Welcome Center and Museum Store, 164

Historic St. Mary's City, 200

Holocaust Memorial Museum. See U.S. Holocaust Memorial Museum

Homestead Farm, 75, 198

Howard B. Owens Science Center and Planetarium, 93

Huntington Museum. See Bowie Train Station and Huntington Museum

Huntley Meadows Park, 68

I

Imagination Stage, 115, 197

Indoor/Outdoor Pools, 151
    Prince Georges County, 151
    Virginia, 151
    Washington DC, 151

International Children's Festival, 126

International Spy Museum, 25

Islamic Center, 26
Iwo Jima Memorial, 53

J

Jefferson District Park and Golf Course, 85
Jefferson Memorial, 10
John Brown Museum. *See* Harpers Ferry National Historical Park
John Brown's Fort. *See* Harpers Ferry National Historical Park
John F. Kennedy Center for the Performing Arts, The, 26, 116
John Poole House, 41
July Fourth Concert at the U.S. Capitol, 115
JW Tumbles, 155

K

Katzen Arts Center/American University Museum, 26
Kenilworth Park and Aquatic Gardens, 77
Kennedy Center. *See* John F. Kennedy Center for the Performing Arts, The
Kennedy Center Family Theater, 199
Kennedy Shriver Aquatic Center, 146
Kettler Capitals IcePlex, 138
Keys. *See* Frederick Keys
Kinder Haus Toys, 131
King Jr., Martin Luther, Memorial, 11
King, Jr., Martin Luther, Swim Center, 147
Kings Dominion. *See* Paramount's Kings Dominion
Kiparoo Farms, 98
Knoebels Amusement Park and Resort, 192
Korean War Veterans Memorial, 10
Koshland Science Museum, 27
Kreeger Museum, The, 27

L

Ladew Topiary Gardens, 171
Lake Accotink Park, 86
Lake Anna State Park, 184
Lake Artemesia Park, 64
Lake Fairfax Park, 86
Lake Frank, 64
Lake Needwood, 65
Land of Little Horses, The, 193

Lane Manor Splash Park, 147
Larriland Farm, 75
LaserNation/UltraZone, 158
Laser Quest, 158
Lawrence, Ellanor C., Park. *See* Walney Visitor Center/Ellanor C. Lawrence Park
Lee District Park and Robert E. Lee Recreation Center, 86
Lee-Fendall House Museum, The, 54
Lee, Robert E., Memorial. *See* Arlington House/The Robert E. Lee Memorial
Lee, Robert E., Recreation Center. *See* Lee District Park and Robert E. Lee Recreation Center
Leesburg Animal Park, 185
Lewis, Reginald F., Museum of Maryland African-American History and Culture, 175
Lexington Market, 172
Liberty Mountain Resort & Conference Center, 143
Library of Congress, 19
Lincoln Cottage/President Lincoln and Soldiers' Home National Monument, 27
Lincoln Memorial, 10
Lincoln Museum. *See* Ford's Theatre, Lincoln Museum, Petersen House
Little Bennett Regional Park, 65
Little Gym, The, 155
Locust Grove Nature Center, 93
Long Branch Nature Center, 93
Luray Caverns, 185
Lyceum, Alexandria's History Museum, The, 54, 200

M

Madame Tussauds DC, 28
Manassas National Battlefield Park, 74
MARC Trains, 6
Marietta House Museum, 41
Marine Barracks Evening Parade, 116
Marine Corps. *See* National Museum of the Marine Corps
Market Square/Alexandria City Hall, 54
Marvatots 'n' Teens, 156
Maryland Hall for the Creative Arts, 116
Maryland Historical Society, 172
Maryland Science Center, 172, 202
Maryland Tourism, 2

Mason District Park, 69

Max Brenner, 161

McCrillis Gardens and Gallery, 77

Meadowbrook Stables, 107

Meadowlark Botanical Gardens, 78

Meadowside Nature Center, 94

Metrorail and Metrobus, 6

Military Band Summer Concerts, 117

Monster Mini Golf, Gaithersburg, 109

Montgomery College Robert E. Parilla
    Performing Arts Center, 117

Montgomery County Airpark, 42

Montgomery County Recreation Outdoor
    Pools MD, 148

Monticello: The Home of Thomas
    Jefferson, 185

Montpelier Mansion, 42

Montrose Park, 87

Mormon Temple. See Washington Temple
    Visitors' Center

Morven Park, 55

Mosaic District Family Events, 117

Mount Vernon Community Children's
    Theatre, 118

Mount Vernon Estate and Gardens
    (George Washington's Home), 55

Mount Vernon Ice Arena, 138

Mount Vernon Trail, 69

Mud Hut, The, 158

My Gym, 156

N

NASA/Goddard Space Flight Center, 42

National Air and Space Museum, 11

National Aquarium in Baltimore, 173, 201

National Arboretum. See U.S. National
    Arboretum

National Archives, 12

National Book Festival, 126

National Building Museum, 28, 201

National Capital Trolley Museum, 43

National Cathedral. See Washington
    National Cathedral

National Cemetery. See Arlington
    National Cemetery

National Children's Museum, 43

National Colonial Farm, 99

National Cryptologic Museum and
    National Vigilance Park, 44

National Firearms Museum, 55

National Gallery of Art, 12
    Sculpture Garden Ice-Skating Rink, 140

National Gallery of the Arts Film
    Program, 118

National Geographic Society. See Explorers
    Hall, National Geographic Society

National Harbor, 44

National Jewish Museum. See B'nai B'rith
    Klutznick National Jewish Museum

National Mall, The, 7
    Constitution Gardens, 8
    Hirshhorn Museum and Sculpture
        Garden, 9
    Jefferson Memorial, 10
    Korean War Veterans Memorial, 10
    Lincoln Memorial, 10
    Martin Luther King Jr. Memorial, 11
    National Air and Space Museum, 11
    National Archives, 12
    National Gallery of Art, 12
    National Museum of African Art, 13
    National Museum of American
        History, 13
    National Museum of Natural History, 13
    National Museum of the American
        Indian, 14
    Roosevelt, Franklin Delano, Memorial, 8
    Smithsonian Institution Information
        Center, 14
    U.S. Botanic Garden, 15
    Vietnam Veterans Memorial, 15
    Washington Monument, 17
    White House, 17

National Museum of African Art, 13

National Museum of American History, 13

National Museum of Civil War
    Medicine, 180

National Museum of Dentistry, 174

National Museum of Health and Medicine
    of the Armed Forces, 44

National Museum of Natural History, 13

National Museum of the American
    Indian, 14

National Museum of the Marine Corps, 186

National Museum of Women in the Arts, 28

National Portrait Gallery, 29

National Postal Museum, 19

Nationals. *See* Potomac Nationals; *See* Washington Nationals

National Shrine of the Immaculate Conception. *See* Basilica of the National Shrine of the Immaculate Conception

National Theatre, The, 118

National Wildlife Visitor Center, Patuxent Research Refuge, 94

National Zoo, 29, 198
  Concerts, 119

Natural History. *See* National Museum of Natural History

Naval Academy. *See* U.S. Naval Academy

Naval Heritage Center. *See* U.S. Navy Memorial and Naval Heritage Center

Naval Observatory. *See* U.S. Naval Observatory

Navy Memorial. *See* U.S. Navy Memorial and Naval Heritage Center

Navy Museum, The, 30

Navy Yard and Art Gallery. *See* Washington Navy Yard and Art Gallery

New Market Battlefield Military Museum, 186

Newseum, 30

Northern Virginia Transportation Commission, 6

Norwood Local Park, 87

Now This! Kids!, 119

Noyes Library for Young Children, 131

O

Oatlands Plantation, 56

Occoquan Regional Park, 87

Octagon, The, 30

Old Bedford Village, 193

Old Post Office Tower, 31

Old Rag Mountain (Shenandoah National Park), 69

Old Stone House, 31

Old Town Trolley Tours (DC), 4

Olney Indoor Swim Center, 148

Olney Manor Skate Park, 139

Olney Theater Center, 120

Orioles. *See* Baltimore Orioles

Oxon Hill Farm, 99

P

Paint Your Own Pottery, 158

Paramount's Kings Dominion, 186

Parent Resource Centers, 156

Parilla, Robert E., Performing Arts Center. *See* Montgomery College Robert E. Parilla Performing Arts Center

Parks. *See* Individual Park Names

Patapsco Valley State Park, 65

Peace Park/Kunzang Palyul Chöling, 95

Petersen House. *See* Ford's Theatre, Lincoln Museum, Petersen House

Phillip Merrill Environmental Center, Chesapeake Bay Foundation, 202

Phillips Collection, The, 31

Pie Sisters, 160

Pink Box Visitors Center, Middleburg, 187

Pirate Adventures on the Chesapeake, 164

Piscataway National Park, 66

Planetarium. *See* Arlington Public Schools Planetarium; *See* Rock Creek Nature Center and Planetarium

Pohick Bay Regional Park and Golf Course, 88

Politics and Prose, 132

Pope-Leighey House. *See* Woodlawn Plantation/Frank Lloyd Wright's Pope-Leighey House

Port Discovery Children's Museum, 174

Portrait Gallery. *See* National Portrait Gallery

Postal Museum. *See* National Postal Museum

Potomac Horse Center, 108

Potomac Nationals, 104

Potomac Overlook Regional Park, 70
  Summer Concert Series, 120

Potomac Riverboat Company Cruises, 4

Potomac Vegetable Farms, 76

Prince George's Publick Playhouse for the Performing Arts, 120

Prince William Forest Park, 70

Publick Playhouse for the Performing Arts. *See* Prince George's Publick Playhouse for the Performing Arts

Public Transportation, 5

Puppet Company Playhouse, 121

Q

Quiet Waters Park, 165

R

Radio and Television Museum, 45
Railroad Museum. *See* Baltimore and Ohio Railroad Museum
Ratner, Dennis and Philip, Museum, The, 40
Ravens. *See* Baltimore Ravens
Red Rock Wilderness Overlook Regional Park, 70
Redskins. *See* Washington Redskins
Renwick Gallery, 32
Reston Ice Skating Pavilion, 139
Ride-On Buses (Montgomery County, MD), 6
Riley House. *See* Uncle Tom's Cabin
Ripken, Cal, Collegiate Baseball League. *See* Cal Ripken Collegiate Baseball League
Riverbend Park, 71
River Farm Garden Park, 78
Rock Creek Nature Center and Planetarium, 95
Rock Creek Park, 60
Rock Creek Park Horse Center, 108
Rockville Ice Arena, 139
Rockville Municipal Swim Center, 149
Rockville Skate Park at Welsh Park, 140
Rockville Town Square Ice Rink, 140
Rocky Gap State Park, 181
Rocky Gorge 4 Seasons Golf Fairway, 109
Rollingcrest-Chillum Splash Pool, 149
Roosevelt, Franklin Delano, Memorial, 8
Roosevelt (Theodore) Island. *See* Theodore Roosevelt Island
Round House Theatre, 121
Roundtop Mountain Resort, 143
Rust Sanctuary (Audubon Naturalist Society), 96

S

Sandy Point State Park, 165
Sandy Spring Museum, The, 45, 200
Scotts Run Nature Preserve, 71
Sculpture Garden Ice-Skating Rink, 140
Second Story Books, 132

Senate House and Visitor's Galleries, 2
Seneca Creek State Park, 66
Shadowland, 159
Shakespeare Library. *See* Folger Shakespeare Library
Shakespeare Theatre. *See* Folger Shakespeare Theatre
Shakespeare Theatre Company, 122
Shenandoah National Park, 187. *See also* Old Rag Mountain
Sideling Hill, 181
Silver Spring Ice Skating at Veterans Arena, 141
Six Flags America and Paradise Island Water Park, 182
Skate-N-Fun Zone, 141
SkateQuest, 141
Skyline Caverns, 187
Sligo Creek Park, 66
Smithsonian Art Museum, 32
Smithsonian Discovery Theater, 122, 198
Smithsonian Folklife Festival, 126
Smithsonian Institution Information Center, 3, 14
Smithsonian's Museum of Asian Art. *See* Freer Sackler/The Smithsonian's Museum of Asian Art
South Germantown Recreational Park, 88
Splash Playground and Miniature Golf, 149
South Mountain Creamery, 182
South Mountain Recreation Area, 182
SPAGnVOLA Chocolate Factory Tour, 45
Spirit. *See* Washington Spirit
Spirit Cruises, 5
Splash Down Water Park, 150
Sportrock Climbing Center, 157
Sports Legends at Camden Yards, 175
Spotsylvania National Military Park. *See* Fredericksburg and Spotsylvania National Military Park
Spy Museum. *See* International Spy Museum
Stabler-Leadbeater Apothecary Shop and Museum, 56
Star-Spangled Banner Flag House, 175
State House Visitor Center, 166
Steven F. Udvar-Hazy Air and Space Center, 56

Stonestreet Museum of 19th Century Medicine. *See* Beall-Dawson House and Stonestreet Museum of 19th Century Medicine

Storer College Museum. *See* Harpers Ferry National Historical Park

Strasburg Railroad, 193

Strathmore, 123

Sugarloaf Mountain, 67

Sullivan's Toy Store, 133

Sully Historic Site, 57

Summit Hall Farm. *See* Bohrer Water Park at Summit Hall Farm

Supreme Court. *See* U.S. Supreme Court

Surratt House Museum, 46

Sweet Lobby, 160

Synetic Theater, 123

T

Temple Hall Farm Regional Park, 99

Textile Museum, 33

The Comedy Spot/Comedy Sportz, 113

Theodore Roosevelt Island, 71

Thomas Sweet, 160

Thompson Boat Center, 107

Thunderbird American Indian Dancers, 199

Toby's Dinner Theatre, 124

Topgolf, 110

Torpedo Factory Art Center, 57

Tours, 3

Toy Castle, 133

Toy Kingdom, 133

Trolley Museum. *See* National Capital Trolley Museum

Tuckahoe Park and Playfield, 88

Tucker Road Ice Rink, 142

Tudor Place, 33

Turtle Park (aka Friendship Park), 89

U

Uncle Tom's Cabin (Riley House/Josiah Henson's Cabin), 46

Underground Railroad Experience Trail, 67

Union Market, 124

Union Station, 34

United. *See* DC United

University of Maryland Observatory, 96

Upton Hill Regional Park, 89

USA Science and Engineering Festival, 127

U.S. Botanic Garden, 15

U.S. Botanic Garden Conservatory, 201

U.S. Holocaust Memorial Museum, 34

U.S. National Arboretum, 79

U.S. Naval Academy, 166

U.S. Naval Observatory, 96

U.S. Navy Memorial and Naval Heritage Center, 34

U.S.S. Constellation, 176

U.S. Supreme Court, 20

V

Vietnam Veterans Memorial, 15

Vigilance Park. *See* National Cryptologic Museum and National Vigilance Park

Virginia Railway Express, 6

Virginia Tourism Corporation, 3

Visitor's Bureaus, 1

Volcano Island Water Park, 150

W

Wakefield Park and Recreation Center. *See* Audrey Moore/Wakefield Park and Recreation Center

Walkersville Southern Railroad, 183

Walney Visitor Center/Ellanor C. Lawrence Park, 100

Walters Art Gallery, 176

Washington and Old Dominion Railroad Regional Park, 72

Washington Ballet, The, 124

Washington Capitals, 104

Washington, George, Home of. *See* Mount Vernon Estate and Gardens

Washington Harbour Ice Rink, 142

Washington Monument, 17

Washington National Cathedral, 35

Washington Nationals, 105

Washington Navy Yard and Art Gallery, 35

Washington Redskins, 105

Washington Sailing Marina, 107

Washington Spirit, 105

Washington Temple Visitors' Center ("Mormon Temple"), 46

Washington Walks, 5

Washington Wizards, 106

Watermark Cruises, 166

Water Mine Family Swimmin' Hole, 150

Watkins Regional Park, 89

Wax Museum. *See* Madame Tussauds DC

Webb Sanctuary (Audubon Naturalist Society), 97

Western Maryland Scenic Railroad, 183

Wheaton Ice Arena, 142

Wheaton Regional Park, 90

White House, 17

White Oak Duckpin Bowling Lanes, 153

White's Ferry, 47

Whitetail Resort, 143

William Paca House and Garden, 167

William, Prince, Forest Park. *See* Prince William Forest Park

Wisp Resort, 144

Wizards. *See* Washington Wizards

Wolf Trap, 125

Women in the Arts. *See* National Museum of Women in the Arts

Woodend Nature Sanctuary (Audubon Naturalist Society), 97

Woodland Horse Center, 108

Woodlawn Plantation/Frank Lloyd Wright's Pope-Leighey House, 57

Woodrow Wilson House, 36

World Trade Center "Top of the World", 176

Wright, Frank Lloyd. *See* Woodlawn Plantation/Frank Lloyd Wright's Pope-Leighey House

X

XP Laser Sport, 159

Z

Zoo. *See* National Zoo; *See* Baltimore Zoo, The

ZooAmerica, North American Wildlife Park, 194